REVISED & EXPANDED
FEATURES UPDATED EXCHANGE VALUES

FAST FOOD FACTS

Nutritive and Exchange Values for Fast-Food Restaurants

Marion J. Franz, R.D., M.S.

WELLNESS & NUTRITION LIBRARY

DCI Publishing

Library of Congress Cataloging-in-Publication Data
Franz, Marion J.
Fast food facts.

1. Convenience foods—Composition—Tables. 2. Food—Composition—Tables.
3. Diabetes—Nutritional aspects. 4. Fast food restaurants—United States.
I. Title.
TX551.F74   1990   613.2'8   90-3063
ISBN 0-937721-67-0

Edited by: Donna Hoel
Cover & Text Design: MacLean & Tuminelly
Photography: Paul Lundquist
Production Manager: Wenda Johnson
Printed in the United States of America

10 9 8 7 6 5 4 3 2 1

Published by:
DCI Publishing
P.O. Box 739
Wayzata, MN 55391

Table of Contents

Introduction

Eating away from home is a growing trend and is on the rise. According to a Gallup survey for the National Restaurant Association, more than 85 million people (47% of United States adults), ate out or purchased food to go from restaurants on a typical day in June 1988. A 1985 Nationwide Food Consumption Survey reported that 57% of women and 69% of men ate away from home at least once in the previous day, an increase of about 15% over the 1977-78 survey.

Between 1960 and 1985, expenditures for food away from home increased from 26% of the total money spent on food to more than 43%. A large portion of this increase has been spent on fast food. From 1970 to 1980, fast-food sales increased by more than 300%, from $6.5 billion to $23 billion per year. By 1985 consumer spending at fast-food restaurants rose to $51 billion, which is approximately 40% of total annual sales for all US restaurants, or $2 of every $5 spent in restaurants. US consumers spend an average of $200 a year on fast foods.

During the same time, the number of fast-food outlets in the US increased from 30,000 to 140,000. This translates into an estimated 200 customers ordering one or more hamburgers every second—totaling $10 billion annually in sales from burgers alone in fast-food chains!

Fast-food chains are opening new restaurants in suburbs, department stores, schools, parks, industry cafeterias, and military installations. Currently, McDonald's is far and away the biggest of the chains and claims the most visits in a year, followed by Burger King and Wendy's. Trailing the burger chains are the hot sandwich restaurants (Hardee's, Arby's, Roy Rogers) and the leading chicken chains (Kentucky Fried Chicken and Church's).

The demand for convenience and a change in eating habits have contributed to the popularity of fast food. Busy schedules often force people to "eat on the run" and consume smaller, more frequent meals throughout the day with periodic snacking. Eating away from home, particularly at fast-food restaurants, buying take-out foods, and ordering home delivery are characteristic of many Americans today.

Dinner is the most popular meal eaten out. According to the National Restaurant Survey, 23% of all adults patronize restaurants for dinner on a typical day. Lunch is a close second, with 22% of all adults eating out. A smaller number of adults eat breakfast (5%) and between-meal snacks (4%) out.

Meals eaten away from home, particularly at fast-food restaurants, potentially can contribute excess calories, fat, and sodium to the diet and limit intake of calcium, dietary fiber, and vitamins A and C. Excess snacking can lead to a high intake of fat and sugar. On the other hand, snacking can make a positive contribution to nutrient intake.

More important to nutritional adequacy than where and when people eat is how frequently they eat and which foods are actually eaten. Today's lifestyle doesn't need to compromise nutritional status. With careful planning, healthful eating can be achieved regardless of our busy lives.

Today four out of 10 consumers claim to have improved their eating habits in restaurants, according to the National Restaurant Association Survey. Consumers stated they were using less or no salt (23%), consuming less fat (20%), and eating fewer fried foods (15%) when eating out.

However, discrepancies in consumer behavior continue. The public seemingly behaves incongruously, often saying one thing and doing another, and this is evident when they dine out. Although restaurants offer lighter and healthier fare, people in the restaurant business consistently report there is still an appreciable demand for "all you can eat" specials and for high-fat, high-sugar desserts. And although better choices are available, consumers consider eating out a "treat" and are reluctant to take advantage of the healthier choices.

Increased consumption of food away from home and increased consumer interest in health, fitness, and nutrition are two trends that seem to be incompatible. The goal of this book is to help you attain the second while still recognizing the first.

Fast Food Can Make Good Nutrition Difficult

People eat $51 billion a year of fast food without knowing what it's composed of. The overall nutrition picture depends on selections of food and serving sizes. For most people, an occasional fast-food meal will not upset an otherwise well-balanced diet. People who eat fast food regularly, especially families with children, need to choose menu selections with more care.

The negative dietary impact associated with fast foods is not because they are devoid of nutrients. In fact, substantial amounts of nutrients are available even at restaurants with limited menus. The best nutritional feature of many fast foods is the protein content. They also provide vitamins and minerals in moderate to large quantities. However, poor choices by consumers and limited variety at some restaurants may pose a problem for those who eat large numbers of fast-food meals each week.

Fast foods may provide ample protein and some vitamins and minerals, but they also tend to provide large amounts of saturated fat, cholesterol, and sodium, not to mention calories. You can easily gulp down half the total number of calories your body needs each day plus all your sodium allotment from a single fast-food meal. For example, if you have a fried fish sandwich, a milk shake, and french fries you've consumed 1,142 calories, 1,425 milligrams of sodium, and 53 grams of fat—with fat making up 42% of the calories.

On a day in which all food selections are obtained from fast-food restaurants, the recommended levels for dietary fat, cholesterol, and sodium are usually exceeded. Despite the recent addition of salads and skim and lowfat milks at several fast-food chains, the selections remain relatively limited. Hence, people who eat all of a day's meals in fast-food restaurants have difficulty meeting all the dietary guidelines (see following example).

In a hurry? Choosing fast foods for all three meals in one day could add up to the following calories:

	Calories	Fat (gm.)	Sodium (mg.)
Breakfast:			
Biscuit w/Sausage, Egg	529	35	1250
Mid-Morning Coffee:			
Doughnut	150	7	139
Lunch:			
Quarter Pounder w/Cheese	517	29	1150
French Fries	312	16	155
Coke, 12 ounces	155	0	6
Dinner:			
Chicken Dinner	885	51	1918
Whole Milk	150	8	120
Evening Snack:			
Large Cone	325	16	75
Total	3023	162	4813

This adds up to 32 teaspoons of fat (48% of total calories) and about 2 teaspoons of salt. The goal is approximately 60 to 90 grams (12 to 18 teaspoons of fat) and less than 3,300 milligrams of sodium daily!

The next chart illustrates that fast foods can be healthful when foods are carefully selected. To make wise food choices you need some knowledge of food composition and preparation techniques. A balanced diet contains a wide variety of foods, some of which may not be found in fast foods. Daily physical exercise is also important to maintaining a good dietary health program.

	Calories	Fat (gm.)	Sodium (mg.)	Exchanges
Breakfast:				
Scrambled Eggs	157	11	290	2 med. fat meat
English Muffin w/ 1 pat butter	169	5	270	2 starch, 1 fat
Grapefruit Juice, 6 oz.	80	-	-	1 fruit
Lowfat Milk, 8 oz.	90	1	120	1 milk
Lunch:				
Chili-Cheese Potato	510	20	610	4 starch, 1 1/2 med. fat meat, 2 fat
Diet Coke	1	0	8	Free
Dinner:				
Chicken Breast Fillet on whole grain bun	340	12	565	2 starch, 3 lean meat
Salad, 2 c.	20	-	20	1 vegetable
Lo-cal Italian Dressing, 2 tbsp.	70	6	100	1 fat
Pineapple Chunks, 1/2 c.	70	tr	0	1 fruit
Total	1507	55	1983	

This adds up to half the calories shown on the first chart—11 teaspoons of fat (33% of total calories) and about 1 teaspoon of salt, meeting the goals of 12 to 18 teaspoons of fat and 1 teaspoon of salt daily.

Calories

The greatest nutrition problem with typical fast foods is usually the high number of calories. Sample meals can range from an appropriate level of 400 to 500 calories to a grand total of 1,400 to 1,500 calories! A quarter-pound burger with cheese, fries, and a shake contain about 1,217 calories, which is considerably more than most dinners prepared at home. This meal contains 56 grams of fat (42% of the total calories)—about 49% of the daily calories needed to maintain the weight of a 165-pound man and 70% of the calories needed by a 128-pound woman. For someone on a diet, 1,217 calories is almost the total portion of the entire day's allowance. Teenage boys can consume high-calorie meals without much of a problem, but the rest of us cannot afford to eat so much of one day's calorie allotment in one meal.

Where do all of the calories in fast foods come from? Fat. Fat (specifically saturated fat, which can contribute to heart disease) and sugar provide most of the calories in fast foods without providing any of the other important nutrients, such as vitamins and minerals.

Fat

On the average, 40 to 60% of calories in fast foods come from fat. Major components such as cheese, mayonnaise, and the popular method of deep fat frying are rich sources of fat. To top it off, many restaurants fry foods in highly saturated beef fat that contains high levels of cholesterol.

Frying increases calorie content significantly, since fats are the most concentrated source of calories. The fat content of hamburgers can range from 10 to 42 grams (90 to 378 calories). The fat content of fried chicken (per piece) ranges from 17 to 26 grams (153 to 234 calories). Most fat in fast foods is of animal origin and is predominantly of the saturated type.

Look for restaurants that have switched to unsaturated vegetable oil instead of animal/vegetable shortenings that contain beef tallow. Before 1985, the biggest chains—including Arby's, Burger King, Hardee's, McDonald's, and Wendy's—were frying potatoes, chicken nuggets, and other fare in beef fat. Since then Burger King, Hardee's, Kentucky Fried Chicken, McDonald's, and Wendy's switched to 100% vegetable oil for cooking everything but french fries. Fries are often still cooked in a blend of beef fat and vegetable oil. The companies say customers prefer the taste of potatoes cooked that way. But today, Hardee's and Kentucky Fried Chicken also fry french fries in vegetable oil.

Chicken and fish items are often thought of as the best choices at fast-food restaurants because they're traditionally lower in calories and fat than beef or other red meats. However, these choices may be worse than the beef because they're usually coated with batter and deep-fried. The batter acts as a sponge, absorbing large amounts of fat during the frying process, so chicken and fish products may, in the end, contain more fat and calories than a hamburger or roast beef sandwich. You can usually order a roast beef sandwich AND fries for less fat than you get in a fried chicken breast sandwich alone!

Sugar

Sugar is added to food to improve taste as well as appearance. The greatest source of sugar is soft drinks and shakes. In 1985, the average American drank 484 12-ounce cans of soda pop, each can containing 8 to 11 teaspoons of sugar. Shakes also get most of their 350 to 400 calories from sugar. A typical small (10-oz) shake contains about as much sugar as a 12-ounce can of regular soda pop (9 to 11 teaspoons), with 2 to 4 teaspoons of fat. A 14-ounce shake has 760 calories, and a 20-ounce shake has 990 calories.

Protein

Most fast-food meals supply 50 to 100% of the protein needed by adults. Even a small hamburger supplies 20% of the Recommended Daily Allowance (RDA) for protein for an adult man and 25% for a woman or child.

Vitamins

Most fast-food meals provide adequate amounts of B vitamins, thiamine, riboflavin, and niacin, as well as vitamins B-6 and B-12. Vitamin C is found in orange juice (served with breakfasts), coleslaw, and salad bars as well as in potatoes.

Minerals

Milk and shakes available in most fast-food outlets are high in calcium and phosphorus. Red meats are excellent sources of iron and zinc.

Sodium

Some menu items also contain large amounts of sodium (salt), which can contribute to high blood pressure. The average American easily eats 10 to 60 times the sodium needed per day.

Several fast-food sandwiches contain 1,500 to 2,000 milligrams of sodium (2/3 to 3/4 teaspoon of salt), more than half the daily recommended maximum sodium intake of not more than 3,300 milligrams (1 to 1 1/2 teaspoons of salt). For instance, a single cheeseburger can contain 1,400 milligrams of sodium and a fish dinner more than 2,000 milligrams. The sodium level of a fast-food meal rises quickly if the consumer selects salted french fries, onion rings, or a milk shake. In addition, condiments such as pickles, catsup, and mustard also contain substantial amounts of sodium.

It's difficult to know by taste how much sodium is in food. Surprisingly, french fries can be the lowest. Salt is sprinkled on before and after frying, which makes the fries taste salty, but the sodium level is lower than that of many other menu items and much of the added salt stays on the paper container!

To their credit, Mcdonald's reduced the amount of sodium in their food items by an average of 15% between 1984 and 1985. However, an Egg McMuffin still contains 740 milligrams of sodium and the new McD.L.T. has 1,170 milligrams of sodium, so there is still plenty of room for improvement.

Fiber

Fast foods, except for salads and coleslaw (recent additions to fast-food menus), are frequently low in fiber. Sources of fiber, such as fruits, vegetables, and whole grains, have not been traditional fast-food offerings. The average American consumes 10 to 20 grams of dietary fiber per day, but the recommended intake is twice that level.

Making Good Fast-Food Choices

What kind of advice can we give to help you make good choices when eating fast foods? Americans should try to eat a variety of foods in moderate portions, with no more than 30% of the daily calories from fat and no more than 3,300 milligrams of sodium. They should eat plenty of high-fiber food and little high-sugar food.

What does this translate into when selecting healthy meals from fast foods? First of all, a prudent eating pattern should contain only enough calories to maintain weight no higher than 10% above the desirable weight for any person's height and body frame. For most women this will be between 1,500 and 1,800 calories per day and for most men between 2,400 and 2,800 calories per day. This means women will be looking for meals that have between 500 and 600 calories, men between 800 and 900 calories.

For women, 30% of calories from fat translates into not more than 60 grams of fat per day, or approximately 20 to 25 grams per meal. For men, it's 90 grams of fat per day, or approximately 30 to 35 grams per meal.

When figuring sodium intake, the goal is to try and stay under 1,000 milligrams per meal.

To summarize, look for meals that meet these guidelines:

	Women	Men
Calories, total meal	500-600	800-900
Fat, grams per meal	20-25	30-35
Sodium, milligrams per meal	1,000	1,000

Let's look at some usual menu items and see if selections can be made to meet these goals.

Burgers

It's a good idea to select basic meat items and scale down to single patties. For a lower-fat sandwich, have a regular hamburger (or even two plain burgers) instead of a double burger with cheese or special sauces, especially the mayonnaise-based sauces. If you've got a double-decker appetite, pile on lettuce and tomato. Cheese adds 100 calories a slice as well as extra fat and sodium, and you can save nearly 150 calories by having them hold the mayo.

Scaling down to single patties can also help avoid protein overload. Super-size burgers can give you about two-thirds of your daily protein requirements in a single meal.

A big, deluxe hamburger, large fries, and large chocolate chip cookie add up to 1,199 calories with 64 grams of fat (48%) and 1,385 milligrams of sodium. Compare this to a regular roast beef sandwich, regular fries, and diet soda at 568 calories with 25 grams of fat (39%) and 704 milligrams of sodium. The following chart gives examples of burger meal choices that meet recommended dietary guidelines.

Burgers

	Calories	Fat (gm.)	Sodium (mg.)	Exchanges
Burger King: Whopper Jr.	322	17	486	2 starch, 2 med. fat meat, 1 fat
Salad Bar w/ Reduced Calorie Dressing	58	2	893	1 vegetable, 1/2 fat
Total	380	19	1379*	

Note high sodium content

	Calories	Fat (gm.)	Sodium (mg.)	Exchanges
Hamburger	275	12	509	2 starch, 2 med. fat meat
French Fries, regular	227	13	160	1 1/2 starch, 2 fat
Total	502	25	669	
Carl's Jr:				
Happy Star Hamburger	220	8	445	2 starch, 1 med. fat meat
Lite Potato w/ 2 tbsp. sour cream	295	5	50	3 1/2 starch, 1 fat
Total	515	13	495	
Dairy Queen:				
Single Hamburger w/ lettuce, tomato	360	16	630	2 starch, 2 med. fat meat, 1 fat
Small Cone	140	4	45	1 1/2 starch, 1 fat
Total	500	20	695	
Hardee's:				
Cheeseburger	310	13	681	2 starch, 1 1/2 med. fat meat, 1 fat
Side Salad	19	1	14	1 starch/vegetable
Cool Twist Cone Vanilla	192	6	89	2 starch, 1 fat
Total	521	20	784	

	Calories	Fat (gm.)	Sodium (mg.)	Exchanges
McDonald's:				
Hamburger	257	10	460	2 starch, 1 med. fat meat
French Fries, regular	220	12	110	2 starch, 2 fat
Orange Juice, 6 oz.	80	-	-	1 fruit
Total	557	22	560	
Quarter Pounder	414	21	660	2 starch, 3 med. fat meat, 1 fat
Side Salad w/ Lite Vinaigrette Dressing	57	3	85	1 vegetable, 1/2 fat
Total	486	25	805	
Cheeseburger	308	14	750	2 starch, 1 1/2 med. fat meat, 1 fat
Orange Juice	80	-	-	1 fruit
Soft Serve Cone	144	5	70	1 1/2 starch, 1 fat
Total	532	19	820	
Wendy's:				
Single Hamburger on multi-grain bun w/ lettuce, tomato	350	16	360	2 starch, 3 med. fat meat
Garden Salad	102	5	140	2 vegetable, 1 fat
Total	452	21	500	

Chicken and Fish

Chicken and fish are often perceived as lighter fare than red meat. They start out very healthful, but battering, breading, or deep-frying cancels out their normal, low-fat advantages and turns them into fatty, high-calorie meals. Choose fish and chicken only if it's roasted, unbreaded, grilled, baked, or broiled without fat—resulting in almost half the fat and calories of fried chicken and fish and lower in sodium as well. Deep-fried chicken items often have the highest calories on a menu. Chicken sandwiches average 500 to 700 calories, including 4 to 6 1/2 fat exchanges. A fish filet sandwich has 400 to 500 calories, including 4 fat exchanges.

Choosing certain fish types over others is another calorie saver: scallops and shrimp are lower in overall fat and calories then fried clams, which have a bigger surface area—hence more fat is absorbed on the coating while frying.

If fried is your only choice, choose regular coating over extra crispy varieties (which soak up more oil during cooking) and save as much as 86 calories per piece. (For instance, Kentucky Fried Chicken's Extra Crispy contains 1 to 2 teaspoons more fat per piece than Original Recipe.) Even better, peel off the skin and lose 100 calories plus most of the fat and excess sodium (coatings tend to be highly seasoned and salted). By ordering separate pieces instead of combinations or whole dinners, you save calories as well. Order mashed potatoes instead of fries and save some 200 calories.

McDonald's chicken sandwich and chicken nuggets have more than 50% of their calories from fat—putting them in the same ballpark as the Big Mac, McNuggets, and Filet-0-Fish sandwich—and have about twice as much fat as the regular hamburger.

If you want chicken nuggets, skip the honey sauce and save 50 calories, avoid the hot-mustard, barbecue, or the sweet-and-sour sauce and save 60 calories or more. Also, skip the tartar sauce (about 120 calories for 2 tablespoons) and use cocktail sauce (only 34) or lemon juice (zero) instead.

The best meal fillers are coleslaw and corn on the cob or a tossed salad and roll (skip the butter and save another 100 calories). If you can find a roasted chicken breast sandwich on a menu (one that is not deep fried), you're in luck. It'll be lower in fat and calories than other menu items. The following chart gives examples of chicken and fish meal choices that meet recommended dietary guidelines.

Chicken and Fish

	Calories	Fat (gm.)	Sodium (mg.)	Exchanges
Arby's:				
Roasted Chicken (Boneless Breast)	254	7	930	6 lean meat
Rice Pilaf	123	2	438	1 1/2 starch
Scandinavian Vegetables in Sauce	56	2	465	2 vegetable
Total	433	11	1833*	
Roasted Chicken (Boneless Leg)	319	16	995	6 lean meat
Baked Potato w/ 2 tbsp sour cream	335	22	62	4 starch, 1 fat
Total	654	38	1057	
Burger King:				
Chicken Tenders	204	10	636	1 starch, 2 med. fat meat
French Fries, regular	227	13	160	1 1/2 starch, 2 fat
Salad Bar w/ Reduced Calorie Italian Salad Dressing	58	2	870	1 vegetable, 1/2 fat
Total	489	25	1666*	
Carl's Jr:				
Charbroiler BBQ Chicken	320	5	955	2 1/2 starch, 3 lean meat
Lite Potato w/ 2 tbsp. sour cream	250	5	85	3 1/2 starch
Total	570	10	1040	

*Note *high sodium content*

	Calories	Fat (gm.)	Sodium (mg.)	Exchanges
Chick-Fil-A:				
Chick-Fil-A Sandwich	426	9	1174	2 1/2 starch, 5 lean meat
Carrot-Raisin Salad	116	5	8	1 fruit, 1 vegetable, 1 fat
Total	542	14	1182*	
Hearty Breast of Chicken Soup (medium)	230	5	890	1 starch, 3 lean meat
Orange Juice	82	tr	2	1 fruit
Icedream	134	5	51	1 starch, 1 fat
Total	446	10	943	
Church's Fried Chicken:				
Chicken Breast	278	17	560	1/2 starch, 3 med. fat meat
Corn w/out butter, 1 ear	156	tr	20	2 starch
Total	434	17	580	
Hardee's:				
Chicken Stix, 6 pieces	210	9	678	1 starch, 3 lean meat
French Fries, regular	226	10	83	1 1/2 starch, 2 fat
Total	436	19	761	

*Note high sodium content

	Calories	Fat (gm.)	Sodium (mg.)	Exchanges
Kentucky Fried Chicken:				
Side Breast, Original Recipe	276	17	654	1/2 starch, 3 med. fat meat
Mashed Potatoes w/ Gravy	62	1	297	1 starch
Coleslaw	103	6	171	2 vegetable, 1 fat
Total	441	24	1122*	
Drumsticks, 2 Original Recipe	294	18	538	1/2 starch, 4 med. fat meat
Corn-on-the-Cob	176	3	21	2 starch
Baked Beans	105	1	387	1 starch
Total	575	22	946	
Long John Silvers:				
Baked Fish Dinner w/ Slaw, Mixed Vegetable	387	19	1298*	1 starch, 4 med. fat meat
Shrimp Salad w/ crackers	183	3	658	1 starch, 3 lean meat
Lemon Meringue Pie	200	56	254	2 starch, 1 fat
Total	383	59	912	
Red Lobster:				
Any Fish (5-oz. luncheon portion)	170	10	50	3 lean meats
Baked Potato w/ 1 tsp. butter	274	7	161	3 starch, 1 fat
Tossed Salad w/ 2 tbsp. Low-Cal Dressing	95	6	100	1 fat
Total	539	23	311	

*Note *high sodium content*

	Calories (gm.)	Fat (mg.)	Sodium	Exchanges
McDonald's:				
Chicken McNuggets	288	16	520	1 starch, 2 med. fat meat, 1 fat
Barbeque Sauce	53	tr	340	1 fruit
Side Salad	57	3	85	1 vegetable, 1/2 fat
Lite Viniagrette Dressing	15	1	60	Free
Total	413	20	1005	
Wendy's:				
Chicken Breast Fillet on bun	340	12	565	2 starch, 3 lean meat
Coleslaw (1/2 c.)	160	10	330	1 starch or 2 vegetable, 2 fat
Total	500	22	895	
Fish Fillet on multi-grain bun	350	22	690	3 starch, 2 med. fat meat
Salad w/ 1 tbsp. Reduced Calorie Dressing	110	6	540	1 vegetable, 1 fat
Total	460	28	1230*	

*Note *high sodium content*

Hot Dogs

Super hot dogs with cheese have 7 teaspoons of fat and 580 calories, along with 1,605 milligrams of sodium (more than 1/2 teaspoon of salt). Add a large malt with 1,060 calories—estimated to contain 25 teaspoons of sugar—and you're in trouble. Stick to the single hamburger with lettuce and tomato, a regular frozen cone, and diet soda pop (506 calories, 710 milligrams of sodium).

Sandwiches

Of the various sandwich versions of roast beef, ham-and-cheese, turkey, etc, your best diet strategy is to choose regular and junior sizes over top-of-the-line models. Consider the differences between the small roast beef (220 calories) and the deluxe version (526 calories). You also save by skipping the mayonnaise topping (shaves off at least 100 calories per tablespoon) and choosing lower-fat sandwich fillers (anything that's not fried).

For lunch, consider sandwiches made with whole grain breads and lean meats, such as roast beef, French dip, turkey breast, or lean ham, which are the lowest in fat. But add bacon, cheese, and sauces and you also add calories and fat. Chicken breast (340 calories) or regular roast beef (320 calories) sandwiches are all relatively low in fat.

Be sure to make full use of no- or low-fat extras (salad bars, coleslaw, plain baked potatoes) that check calories and fat and yet make a sandwich meal more complete in nutrients.

Choose roast beef over burgers whenever you can. A roast-beef sandwich packs just as much iron as a Big Mac. A plain roast beef sandwich with no sauce (Arby's, Hardee's, and Roy Rogers) provides fewer calories and is leaner than a hamburger—sometimes 250 fewer calories—with almost as much protein, just as much iron, but only a fraction of the fat. Even with barbecue sauce, a roast beef sandwich puts the big burgers to shame.

Croissant sandwiches are high in calories, fat, and cholesterol—one croissant sandwich averages 400 to 500 calories. Compare this with a whole grain or white bun that has just 135 calories. A plain roast beef sandwich has just 350 calories and a pita sandwich has just 285 calories. The following chart gives examples of sandwich meal choices that meet recommended dietary guidelines.

Sandwiches

	Calories	Fat (gm.)	Sodium (mg.)	Exchanges
Arby's:				
Roast Beef, regular	353	15	590	2 starch, 2 med. fat meat, 1 fat
French Fries, regular	215	10	114	2 starch, 2 fat
Total	568	25	704	

	Calories	Fat (gm.)	Sodium (mg.)	Exchanges
Hot Ham'n Cheese	292	14	1350	1 starch, 3 med. fat meat
Potato Cakes	201	13	397	1 1/2 starch, 2 fat
Total	493	27	1747*	
Turkey Deluxe	375	17	1047	2 starch, 3 med. fat meat
Tossed Salad w/ Low-Cal Italian Dressing	57	1	465	1 vegetable
Total	432	18	1512	
Carl's Jr: Charbroiler BBQ Chicken	320	5	955	3 1/2 starch, 3 lean meat
Lite Potato w/ 2 tbsp. sour cream	295	5	85	3 1/2 starch, 1 fat
Total	615	10	1040	
California Roast Beef 'N Swiss	360	8	1070	3 starch, 3 lean meat
Old-Fashioned Chicken Noodle Soup	80	1	605	1 starch
Total	440	9	1675*	

*Note high sodium content

	Calories	Fat (gm.)	Sodium (mg.)	Exchanges
Hardee's:				
Roast Beef	338	15	966	2 starch, 2 med. fat meat, 1 fat
Side Salad w/ 2 tbsp. Reduced Calorie Dressing	65	5	93	1 vegetable, 1 fat
Total	403	20	1059	
Hot Ham 'N Cheese	316	10	1497	2 starch, 2 med. fat meat
Side Salad w/ 2 tbsp. Reduced Calorie Dressing	65	5	93	1 vegetable, 1 fat
Total	381	15	1590*	
Jack in the Box:				
Club Pita w/out Sauce	277	8	931	2 starch, 2 lean meat
Side Salad	51	3	84	1 lean meat
Reduced Calorie French Dressing (2 tbsp.)	80	4	300	1/2 starch, 1 fat
Total	408	15	1315*	
Rax:				
Roast Beef, regular	320	11	969	2 starch, 2 med. fat meat
Plain Baked Potato	270	11	70	4 starch
1 tbsp liquid margarine	100	—	100	2 fat
Total	690	22	1139*	

*Note high sodium content

	Calories	Fat (gm.)	Sodium (mg.)	Exchanges
Roy Rogers:				
Roast Beef	317	10	785	2 starch, 3 lean meat
Coleslaw	110	7	261	2 vegetable, 1 fat
Total	427	17	1046	
Steak 'N Shake:				
Steakburger	277	7	425	2 starch, 2 lean meat
Baked Beans	173	4	656	2 starch, 1 fat
Total	450	11	1081	

Potatoes and Chili

When it comes to potatoes, a plain baked one is nourishing, filling, and virtually free of fat and sodium. A plain, large potato weighing 10 1/2 ounces provides 250 calories and 2 grams of fat. Adding cheeses, bacon, sour cream, and other toppings can increase the fat level from 2 grams to 30 to 40 grams (6 to 8 teaspoons) and the calories from 250 to 780. The sodium also skyrockets from under 50 to 1,000 milligrams (1/2 teaspoon of salt). A deluxe super-stuffed baked potato with sour cream, butter, bacon, and cheese has 650 calories and 8 teaspoons of fat.

Choose a plain baked potato for lunch or dinner. When combined with a salad and topped with 1/4 cup serving of cottage cheese or 1 tablespoon grated Swiss, cheddar, or Parmesan cheese (from the salad bar), a baked potato becomes a complete meal. Top it with vegetables instead of adding cheese sauces, bacon, sour cream, and other toppings and you save the equivalent of 8 pats of butter—and for the calories saved you can even order a plain hamburger. Even the baked potato with chicken a'la king is a better selection than baked potatoes with fat-laden broccoli and cheese.

If you are trying to cut calories, go easy on the french fries. Split an order with someone else or, better yet, go with the plain baked potato. If the choice is between mashed potatoes and french fries, the better choice is mashed. Even with gravy, they're still lower in fat and calories. If the fries are just too tempting, limit them to a once-in-awhile treat. If it's between fries or onion rings, however, know that breading makes onion rings higher in fat and calories.

Chili blows the typical greasy-spoon reputation. Chili and several restaurant roast beef sandwiches are just about the only fast-food, red-meat dishes that get less than 30% of their calories from fat. Even a large bowl of chili has only 360 calories and 12 grams of fat. Beans are one of the best sources of fiber, making chili with beans, baked beans, and refried beans good choices. At the salad bar, choose kidney beans, garbanzo beans, and fruit for added fiber. Baked potatoes with skins are another good choice for fiber; however, ordering only the skins usually means deep-fat fried skins with salty, fatty toppings.

The following chart gives examples of potato and chili choices that meet recommended dietary guidelines.

Potatoes and Chili

	Calories (gm.)	Fat (mg.)	Sodium	Exchanges
Carl's Jr:				
Broccoli/Cheese Potato	470	17	690	4 starch, 1 med. fat meat, 2 fat
Rax:				
Plain Baked Potato	270	tr	70	4 starch
Chili Topping	80	2	221	1/2 starch, 1 lean meat
Total	350	2	291	

	Calories	Fat (gm.)	Sodium (mg.)	Exchanges
Roy Rogers:				
Potato w/ Broccoli 'n Cheese	376	18	523	3 starch, 1 med. fat meat, 2 fat
Steak'N Shake:				
Chili Mac & 4 Saltines	310	12	1301	2 starch, 1 med. fat meat, 1 fat
Lettuce/Tomato Salad w/ 1/2 oz 1,000 Island Dressing	98	7	115	1 vegetable, 1 1/2 fat
Total	408	19	1416	
Wendy's:				
Baked Potato w/ Chili and Cheese	510	20	610	4 starch, 1 1/2 med. fat meat, 2 fat
Chili, large	360	12	1455	2 starch, 3 med. fat meat
Bread Sticks, 4	70	1	120	1 starch
Total	430	13	1575*	

*Note high sodium content

Pizza

It is by no means regrettable that pizza is becoming a more popular fast-food entree. With a tomato sauce base, mozzarella cheese, and a flour-based crust, pizza offers protein, vitamins, and carbohydrates all in one fairly low-fat package. All this is dependent, however, on the choices you make.

As a snack or part of a quick meal, pizza can fit nicely into a well-balanced diet. It's not necessarily a low-calorie food, but with its calories it also contributes very respectably to nutrition. On average, a serving has about 20 grams of protein—more than one-third of the RDA for most adults. Cheese pizza shines in calcium—an average of about 400 milligrams per slice, or one-half of the RDA. Meat pizza's average 200 milligrams of calcium—35 percent of the RDA. It's also a good source of some B vitamins (in the crust) and vitamins A and C (tomato sauce and vegetable toppings). If you stop with two slices of a small cheese pizza (about 450 calories—24% from fat) you won't do undue damage to your waistline.

Generally the best chance of finding nutritional balance lies with cheese pizza. Top the pizza with mushrooms, green peppers, and onions and you are doing yourself a good turn. However, some upscale pizza parlors may compete by loading their pizza with tons of cheese and toppings. Top the pizza with pepperoni, sausage, anchovies, or extra cheese and you are adding unnecessary fat, sodium, and calories—as much as 170 calories per slice. To avoid additional sodium, skip the olives and anchovies. Opt for a thin-crust over thick and save up to 130 calories per slice.

Add a salad (many pizza places offer salads or have salad bars) to the pizza and the meal is even more well-rounded. To finish the meal and to give you the feeling that you've filled yourself up, bring some fresh fruit for dessert. The following chart gives examples of pizza choices that meet recommended dietary guidelines.

Pizza

	Calories (gm.)	Fat (mg.)	Sodium	Exchanges
Domino's:				
Plain Cheese Pizza 2 slices, 16" large	376	10	483	4 starch, 2 med. fat meat
Ham Pizza 2 slices, 16" large	417	11	805	4 starch, 2 med. fat meat
Godfather's:				
Original 1/4 Cheese medium	540	16	860	4 starch, 3 med. fat meat
Original Cheese Pizza 1/2 mini	380	8	520	4 starch, 1 med. fat meat
Thin Crust Cheese 1/4 medium	420	14	820	4 starch, 2 med. fat meat
Pizza Hut:				
Cheese Thin-N-Crispy 3 slices, 1/2 10"	450	15	**	3 starch, 1 vegetable, 2 med. fat meat, 1 fat
Salad w/ Low-Cal Italian Dressing	95	5	**	2 vegetable, 1 fat
Total	545	20		

** *Not available*

	Calories (gm.)	Fat (mg.)	Sodium	Exchanges
Beef Thin-N-Crispy 3 slices, 1/2 10"	490	19	**	3 starch, 3 med. fat meat, 1 fat
Salad w/ Low-Cal Italian Dressing	95	5	**	
Total	585	24		
Pepperoni Thin-N-Crispy 3 slices, 1/2 10"	430	17	**	3 starch, 2 med. fat meat, 1 fat
Salad w/ Low-Cal Italian Dressing	95	5	**	
Total	525	22		
Shakey's: Thin Cheese, 2/10 of a 12"	266	10	646	2 starch, 2 med. fat meat
Thin Crust w/ onion, green pepper, olive, mushroom 2 slices(10 slices per 12" pizza)	250	10	626	2 starch, 2 med. fat meat

** *Not available*

Salads

According to a Consumer Report survey, about one in seven readers ate a salad the last time they visited a fast-food restaurant. About one in four said they visit fast-food places more often now that salads are available.

To keep fat and calories down, be careful of high-fat toppings, such as regular dressings, bacon, cheeses, seeds, and eggs. A salad from a salad bar averages 80 to 100 calories. Load up on lettuce and fresh vegetables such as carrots, tomatoes, and dark-green vegetables. And go easy on dressings, fatty croutons, taco chips, and those mayonnaise-laden pasta and potato salads. Three tablespoons of regular dressing will add 200 calories, while a reduced-calorie dressing will add about half that amount. Avoid items made with dressings, such as potato, carrot, or macaroni salads, which contain mayonnaise or oil. If watching sodium intake, skip salty bacon bits, pickled vegetables, and croutons. To cut back on sugar, choose fresh fruits instead of canned fruits in heavy syrup.

A large salad containing a variety of vegetables, 1/2 cup cottage cheese, and reduced-calorie salad dressing has less than 250 calories. However, by adding just one tablespoon of regular dressing, some bacon bits, and 1/4 cup macaroni or potato salad, you increase the calorie level to 500. Adding coleslaw (1/2 cup, 90 calories) sunflower seeds, and raisins (1/4 cup, 180 calories), increases it further. The following chart gives examples of salad choices that meet recommended dietary guidelines.

Salads

	Calories (gm.)	Fat (mg.)	Sodium	Exchanges
Burger King:				
Chef Salad	180	11	610	2 vegetable, 1 med. fat meat
Reduced Calorie Italian Dressing, 1 pkg	30	2	870	1/2 fat
Total	210	13	1480*	
Chicken Salad w/out Dressing	140	4	440	1 vegetable, 2 lean meat
Shrimp & Pasta Salad	170	8	280	1 starch, 1 lean meat, 1 fat
Hardee's:				
Chef's Salad	248	15	932	4 lean meat, 1 fat
Chicken Fiesta Salad	286	14	533	1 vegetable, 3 med. fat meat
Jack-in-the-Box:				
Taco Salad	377	24	1436	1/2 starch, 4 med. fat meat, 1 fat
Pasta and Seafood Salad	394	22	1570	2 starch, 2 med. fat meat, 2 fat

Note high sodium content

	Calories (gm.)	Fat (mg.)	Sodium	Exchanges
Long John Silvers:				
Shrimp Salad	183	3	658	1 starch, 3 lean meat
Combo Salad w/ crackers	222	8	1051	1 starch, 3 med. fat meat, 2 fat
Ocean Chef Salad w/ crackers	222	8	983	1 starch, 3 lean meat
McDonald's:				
Chef Salad	231	14	490	1 vegetable, 3 med. fat meat
Shrimp Salad	104	3	480	1 vegetable, 2 lean meat
Chicken Salad Oriental	141	3	230	1 vegetable, 3 lean meat
Rax:				
Garden Salad	160	11	362	1 vegetable, 1 med. fat meat, 1 fat
Lite French Dressing	40	2	122	1 fat
Total	200	13	484	
Chef Salad	230	14	1048	1 vegetable, 3 med. fat meat
Lite Thousand Island	40	3	143	1 fat
Total	270	17	1191*	

Note high sodium content

	Calories (gm.)	Fat (mg.)	Sodium	Exchanges
Roy Rogers:				
A La Carte Salad	233	8	454	1 starch, 1 med. fat meat, 1 vegetable, 1 fat
Wendy's:				
Taco Salad	430	19	1260	3 starch, 2 med. fat meat, 2 fat
Taco Sauce	10	tr	105	Free
Total	440	19	1365*	
Garden Spot Salad Bar:				
Lettuce (Iceberg, Romaine)	20	tr	20	1 vegetable
Carrots, cauliflower, cucumbers, green pepper	19	tr	22	1 vegetable
Reduced Calorie Dressing (1 tbsp)	45	4	180	1 fat
Cottage Cheese, 1/2 c.	110	4	425	2 lean meat
Bread Sticks, 4	70	2	120	1 starch
Total	264	10	767	

Note high sodium content

Mexican

Tacos and tostadas are your best calorie and nutrient picks and are good choices when eating out. Go for bean burritos, soft tacos, or other non-fried items. Even a super taco is a leaner option at less than 300 calories (less than a roast beef sandwich). Spice them to your taste. To keep the fat and calories down, go easy on the cheese and pass on the sour cream and guacamole. Pile on extra tomatoes and salsa.

If you're tempted by the bean- and cheese-covered nachos (approximately 700 calories an order), have a bean-filled burrito instead for half the fat and calories. The following chart gives examples of Mexican food choices that meet recommended dietary guidelines.

Mexican

	Calories (gm.)	Fat (mg.)	Sodium	Exchanges
Jack in the Box:				
Super Taco	288	17	765	1-1/2 starch, 1 med. fat meat, 2 fat
Fajita Pita	278	7	611	2 starch, 2 lean meat
Salsa	8	tr	129	Free
Total	286	7	740	
Chicken Fajita Pita	292	8	703	2 starch, 3 lean meat
Salsa	8	tr	129	Free
Total	300	8	832	
Taco Bell:				
Bean Burrito	359	4	65	3 1/2 starch, 1 med. fat meat, 1 fat
Taco, 2	368	22	548	2 starch, 4 lean meat
Taco Sauce, 1 packet	2	tr	126	Free
Total	370	22	674	
Tostada	243	11	670	2 starch, 1 med. fat meat, 1 fat
Salsa	18	tr	376	Free
Total	261	11	746	

	Calories (gm.)	Fat (mg.)	Sodium	Exchanges
Fajita Steak Taco	235	11	507	1 starch, 2 med. fat meat
Chicken Fajita Pita	292	8	703	2 starch, 3 lean meat
Salsa	8	tr	129	Free
Total	300	8	832	
Chicken Fajita	226	10	619	1 starch, 2 med. fat meat
Zantigo: Taco, 2	396	24	636	2 starch, 2 med. fat meat, 2 fat
Beef Enchilada	315	15	904	1 1/2 starch, 2 med. fat meat, 1 fat

Beverages

Shakes and soft drinks are sources of hidden fats and sugars. Save calories by drinking diet beverages, low-fat milk, fruit juice, or water. Low-fat milk provides much more protein and calcium per calorie than fast-food shakes. Fruit juices are high in vitamin C and are good alternatives to higher calorie sodas and shakes. Or stick with no-cal coffee, tea, diet sodas, and the best of all beverage choices—water.

Desserts

Many fast-food desserts are high in fat and calories, so one option is to satisfy yourself by bringing fresh fruit from home. Try eating your "dessert" fruit first; it's a creative way to curb your appetite and avoid overeating.

Or satisfy your sweet tooth with low-fat frozen yogurt (only 80 calories per 1/3 cup with minimal fat) or a small ice cream cone. A cool twist cone from Hardee's has 164 calories with 5 grams of fat.

Ices, sorbets, and sherbets generally have less fat and fewer calories than ice cream and gelato. Frozen yogurt and reduced-calorie "ice creams" are better health buys—both save calories.

To perk up plain ice cream and still save some calories, ask for chocolate sprinkles (about 34 calories per 1/4 ounce) and skip the hot fudge, sauces, nuts, and whipped toppings. To work ice cream calories into a fast-food meal plan, omit one starch/bread and one tablespoon of butter (2 fat exchanges) at a meal. The following chart gives examples of fast-food dessert choices that meet recommended dietary guidelines.

Desserts

	Calories (gm)	Fat (mg)	Sodium	Exchanges
Church's Fried Chicken:				
Frozen Dessert, 4 oz	180	6	65	2 starch, 1 fat
Colombo:				
Lowfat Frozen Yogurt, 4 oz	99	2	35	1 starch, 1/2 fat
Dairy Queen:				
Small Cone	140	4	45	1 1/2 starch, 1 fat
DQ Sandwich	140	4	40	1 1/2 starch, 1 fat
Hardee's:				
Cool Twist Cone Vanilla	192	6	89	2 starch, 1 fat
McDonald's:				
Soft Serve Cone	144	5	70	1 1/2 starch, 1 fat
Rax:				
Chocolate Chip Cookie	130	6	65	1 starch, 1 fat
TCBY (The Country's Best Yogurt)				
Yogurt, 5 oz.	150	3	65	2 starch
Wendy's:				
Chocolate or Butterscotch Pudding	90	4	70	1 starch

Breakfasts

Choices for a fast-food lunch or dinner may be easier than for breakfast because morning food options tend to be heavier in fat, calories, and cholesterol. For instance, the cholesterol count on egg dishes with bacon, sausage, or ham fillers ranges from 250 to 525 milligrams. Counterbalance by cutting back on eggs the rest of the week. The National Cholesterol Education Program recommends that we eat no more than 300 milligrams daily (about one and a half eggs). Breakfast biscuits contain 500 to 700 calories, 30 to 35 grams of fat, and more than 1,000 milligrams of sodium. Try to order breakfast sandwiches on virtually fat-free English muffins or hamburger buns, because even plain croissants are high in fat—equal to as much as four pats of butter.

Sausage versions of breakfast sandwiches are also generally higher in fat and calories. A sausage and egg biscuit, hash brown potatoes, and large orange juice contribute 820 calories with 49 grams of fat and 1,475 milligrams sodium.

Start your day with plain muffins, biscuits, or toast. Request no butter and use low-sugar jam or jelly instead. Add a fruit juice and lowfat or skim milk. For a fast but healthy breakfast, try a whole grain English muffin or plain toast with a small amount of margarine or butter, lowfat milk, and fruit or fruit juice.

If you order a scrambled egg with an English muffin, the calories total only 366, with 17 grams of fat and 575 milligrams of sodium. This is still a substantial breakfast, but it has less fat, sodium, and calories than many other fast-food breakfasts. Other choices are English muffins with cottage cheese and applesauce, bran cereal with fresh fruit and milk, yogurt and a banana, or apple with peanut butter.

A surprisingly good breakfast option is pancakes without butter. They have less fat than croissants and are relatively cholesterol-free. Bring your own diet jam, jelly, or syrup. The following chart gives examples of breakfast choices that meet recommended dietary guidelines.

Breakfasts

	Calories (gm.)	Fat (mg.)	Sodium	Exchanges
Burger King: Bagel w/ Ham, Egg, Cheese	418	15	1130*	3 starch, 2 med. fat meat, 1 fat
Carl Jr's: Scrambled Eggs	120	9	105	1 med. fat meat, 1 fat
English Muffin w/ margerine	180	6	275	2 starch, 1 fat
Total	300	15	380	

Note high sodium content

	Calories (gm.)	Fat (mg.)	Sodium	Exchanges
Bran Muffins	220	6	300	2 starch, 1 fat
Scrambled Eggs	120	9	105	1 med. fat meat, 1 fat
Total	340	15	405	
Hardee's:				
Ham Biscuit	321	15	1075	2 starch, 1 med. fat meat, 2 fat
McDonald's:				
Egg McMuffin	293	12	740	2 starch, 2 med. fat meat
Orange Juice	80	0	0	1 fruit
Total	373	12	740	
Scrambled Eggs	157	11	290	2 med. fat meat
English Muffin w/ butter	169	5	270	2 starch, 1 fat
Grapefruit Juice	80	0	0	1 fruit
Total	406	16	560	
Wendy's:				
Omelet (mushroom, green pepper, onion)	210	15	200	1 vegetable, 2 med. fat meat, 1 fat
Toast, 2 slices	250	9	410	2 starch, 2 fat
Orange Juice	80	tr	tr	1 fruit
Total	540	24	610	
Whataburger:				
Pancakes w/out Syrup and Butter	288	4	977	3 1/2 starch, 1 fat

To Sum It All Up

Today many fast-food restaurants offer salad bars, low-calorie salad dressings, soups, baked potatoes, baked fish, diet soft drinks, and low-fat milk that can help the calorie-conscious consumer, as well as persons with diabetes, limit calories, fat, and sodium in a fast-food meal.

The key to reducing calories is to buy small and eat only at meal times. The average calorie count of a fast-food meal is 685, which is not outrageously high. However, many people buy fast-food items as snacks rather than meals; the average calorie count for a so-called snack is 427. Added to regular meals, that many calories can put people well over their daily limits. Words on a menu like "jumbo," "giant," or "deluxe" signal diet caution. Larger serving sizes mean not only additional calories, but generally more fat, cholesterol, and sodium.

Make wise food choices. If you have fast foods for one meal, try to balance the rest of your day's food choices. Remember, not only is it important to make healthy selections, it's important to eat all three meals a day, including breakfast and lunch—meals that are tempting to skip because of trying to diet to lose weight, hectic schedules, meetings, etc. Although exercise is important, don't skip lunch in order to find time to exercise. Both are important!

Even the hardest critic of fast food has to admit it's convenient. You don't have to go far or wait long to get fast food. This can be a major advantage, especially if you have a limited time to eat.

If You Have Diabetes

Persons with diabetes will no doubt at times find it convenient or necessary to eat fast foods. When you do, the guidelines in this book can help you make wise decisions. Know your meal plan. You'll need to choose foods that fit into your available exchanges for meals or snacks.

Avoid high-fat, high-sugar, and high-sodium foods. Set your goals for approximately 20 to 25 grams of fat and not more than 1,000 milligrams (1/2 teaspoon of salt) per meal. If weight is a concern, pay special attention to caloric values. You may need to supplement a fast-food meal with some fruit and/or skim milk. Nutritional adequacy can be assured by eating a variety of vegetables, fruits, low-fat milk, and whole grain foods in the rest of your meals and snacks during the day.

By knowing the nutritional value of fast-food items, you can choose foods that will be consistent with your meal plan. Fast-food chains may be easier to predict than some expensive gourmet restaurants. Studies of the leading chains show remarkable uniformity in portion sizes and nutrition value of their foods. This book has been designed to alert you to the nutritive value of food items and their exchange values, thus helping you to make wise food choices.

Fast-Food Nutrient And Exchange Values

The fast-food restaurant lists are divided into three sections: 1) menu items, nutritive values, and suggested exchanges; 2) menu items, nutritive values and suggested exchanges for foods recommended for occasional use only due to their sugar content; 3) menu items and their nutritive values for foods that are not recommended for use because of the large amounts of refined sugar they contain. You may find that many of the foods on the first or second list don't fit into your meal plan either. They may contain too many calories or too much fat and, as a result, the exchange values may be greater than the number you have available in your meal plan.

To help you recognize items with large amounts of fat, a "▤" symbol has been placed in the margin for items with more than 2 fat exchanges per serving. Sodium values in milligrams per serving are included in this book to help you regulate your sodium consumption. A "✗" symbol has been placed in the margin for items with more than 800 milligrams sodium. A "♛" symbol is next to foods that contain moderate to high amounts of sugar.

We've listed nutritive information on many fast-food establishments found in the US and Canada, including calories; grams of carbohydrate, protein, fat, and if available, saturated fat; milligrams of cholesterol; milligrams of sodium; and suggested exchange values. Some of the values are based on actual laboratory analysis and some were calculated from nutrient composition tables. The values indicated are averages and may vary from restaurant to restaurant.

This book was planned to help you make intelligent choices. Good luck!

Marion Franz, MS, RD
Director of Nutrition
International Diabetes Center

The author would like to thank Joelle McCaffrey and Mary Ann Roeder for their help in preparing this information. Thanks also to Cheryl Weiler and Donna Hoel, editors, for pulling it all together.

Products	SERVING SIZE	CALORIES	CARBO-HYDRATE (gm)	PROTEIN (gm)	FAT (gm)	SAT. FAT (gm)	CHOLES-TEROL (mg)	SODIUM (mg)	Exchanges
ARBY'S									
Junior Roast Beef	1 (3 oz.)	218	22	12	9	*	20	345	1½ starch, 1½ med. fat meat
Regular Roast Beef	1 (5.2 oz.)	353	32	22	15	*	39	590	2 starch, 2 med. fat meat, 1 fat
Beef 'n Cheddar	1 (7 oz.)	455	28	26	27	*	63	955	2 starch, 3 med. fat meat, 2 fat
Bac 'n Cheddar Deluxe	1 (8 oz.)	526	33	27	37	*	78	1672	2 starch, 3 med. fat meat, 3 fat
King Roast Beef	1 (6.7 oz.)	467	44	27	19	*	49	765	3 starch, 3 med. fat meat
Super Roast Beef	1 (8.3 oz.)	501	50	25	22	*	40	800	3 starch, 3 med. fat meat, 1 fat
Chicken Breast Sandwich	1 (6.9 oz.)	509	36	26	29	*	83	1082	2½ starch, 3 med. fat meat, 2 fat
Hot Ham 'n Cheese Sandwich	1 (5.5 oz.)	292	19	23	14	*	45	1350	1 starch, 3 med. fat meat
Turkey Deluxe	1 (7 oz.)	375	33	24	17	*	39	1047	2 starch, 3 med. fat meat
Fish Fillet Sandwich	1 (7.4 oz.)	580	51	22	32	*	70	928	3 starch, 2 med. fat meat, 4 fat
Philly Beef 'n Swiss	1 (7 oz.)	460	27	24	28	*	107	1300	2 starch, 3 med. fat meat, 2 fat
Roasted Chicken Boneless Breast	1 (5 oz.)	254	2	43	7	*	200	930	6 lean meat
Roasted Chicken Boneless Leg	1 (5.35 oz.)	319	1	41	16	*	214	995	6 lean meat
Rice Pilaf	1 (4 oz.)	123	23	3	2	*	0	438	1½ starch
Scandinavian Vegetables in Sauce	1 (4 oz.)	56	9	2	2	*	0	465	2 vegetable
Chicken Salad Sandwich	1 (5.2 oz.)	386	33	18	20	*	30	630	2 starch, 2 med. fat meat, 2 fat
Chicken Club Sandwich	1 (7 oz.)	621	57	26	32	*	108	1300	4 starch, 2 med. fat meat, 4 fat
Chicken Salad & Croissant	1 (5 oz.)	472	16	22	36	*	12	725	1 starch, 3 med. fat meat, 4 fat

目 = More than 2 fat exchanges per serving   ⫪ = More than 800 milligrams sodium   🛒 = High amounts of sugar

Products	SERVING SIZE	CALORIES	CARBO-HYDRATE (gm)	PROTEIN (gm)	FAT (gm)	SAT. FAT (gm)	CHOLES-TEROL (mg)	SODIUM (mg)	Exchanges
☷ Chicken Salad w/Tomato & Lettuce	1 (9 oz.)	515	24	25	36	*	12	745	1 starch, 1 vegetable, 3 med. fat meat, 4 fat
Tossed Salad, Plain	1 (7 oz.)	44	7	3	tr	*	0	23	1 vegetable
Tossed Salad w/Low Calorie Italian Dressing	1 (8 oz.)	57	8	3	1	*	0	465	1 vegetable
Baked Potato, Plain	1 (11 oz.)	290	66	8	1	*	0	12	4 starch
☷ Superstuffed Potato Deluxe	1 (11 oz.)	648	59	18	38	*	72	475	4 starch, 1 high fat meat, 5 fat
☷ Superstuffed Potato Broccoli & Cheddar	1 (12 oz.)	541	72	13	22	*	24	475	4 starch, 1 vegetable, 1 high fat meat, 3 fat
☷ Superstuffed Potato Mushroom & Cheese	1 (10.5 oz.)	506	61	16	22	*	21	635	4 starch, 1 high fat meat, 3 fat
Superstuffed Potato Taco	1 (15 oz.)	619	73	23	27	*	145	1065	5 starch, 2 high fat meat, 2 fat
French Fries	1 (2.5 oz.)	215	30	2	10	*	8	114	2 starch, 2 fat
Potato Cakes	1 (3 oz.)	201	20	2	13	*	13	397	1½ starch, 2 fat

NOT RECOMMENDED FOR USE

Products	SERVING SIZE	CALORIES	CARBO-HYDRATE (gm)	PROTEIN (gm)	FAT (gm)	SAT. FAT (gm)	CHOLES-TEROL (mg)	SODIUM (mg)	Exchanges
♡ Vanilla Shake	8.8 oz.	295	44	8	10	*	30	245	
♡ Chocolate Shake	10.6 oz.	384	62	9	11	*	32	300	
♡ Jamocha Shake	10.8 oz.	424	76	8	10	*	31	280	

BONANZA RESTAURANTS

Products	SERVING SIZE	CALORIES	CARBO-HYDRATE (gm)	PROTEIN (gm)	FAT (gm)	SAT. FAT (gm)	CHOLES-TEROL (mg)	SODIUM (mg)	Exchanges
Chicken Monterey	4 oz. skinless 1 oz. sauce	152	3	22	5	*	47	332	3 lean meat
Ribeye	5.5 oz.	196	1	28	8	*	50	563	4 lean meat
Halibut	6 oz.	139	3	26	2	*	60	128	3 lean meat

Products	SERVING SIZE	CALORIES	CARBO-HYDRATE (gm)	PROTEIN (gm)	FAT (gm)	SAT. FAT (gm)	CHOLES-TEROL (mg)	SODIUM (mg)	Exchanges
BURGER KING									
Hamburger	1	275	29	15	12	5	37	509	2 starch, 2 med. fat meat
Cheeseburger	1	317	30	17	15	7	48	651	2 starch, 2 med. fat meat, 1 fat
Whopper Sandwich	1	628	46	27	36	12	90	880	3 starch, 3 med. fat meat, 4 fat
Whopper w/Cheese	1	711	47	32	43	17	113	1164	3 starch, 4 med. fat meat, 4 fat
Whopper Jr.	1	322	30	15	17	6	41	486	2 starch, 2 med. fat meat, 1 fat
Whopper Jr. w/Cheese	1	364	31	17	20	2	52	628	2 starch, 2 med. fat meat, 2 fat
Bull's Eye Barbecue Burger	1	638	49	36	33	15	106	1046	3 starch, 4 med. fat meat, 2 fat
Bacon Double Cheeseburger	1	510	27	33	31	15	104	728	2 starch, 4 med. fat meat, 2 fat
Whaler Fish Sandwich	1	488	45	19	27	6	77	592	3 starch, 2 med. fat meat, 3 fat
Ham & Cheese Specialty Sandwich	1	471	44	24	23	9	70	1534	3 starch, 3 med. fat meat, 1 fat
Chicken Specialty Sandwich	1	688	56	26	40	8	82	1423	4 starch, 2 med. fat meat, 5 fat
Chicken Tenders	6 pieces	204	10	20	10	2	47	636	1 starch, 2 med. fat meat
Chicken Bundles	1 order	410	35	14	23	5	8	729	2 starch, 1 med. fat meat, 4 fat
Chicken Bundles with Cheese	1 order	470	36	17	28	9	17	942	2 starch, 2 med. fat meat, 4 fat
Burger Bundles	Serving of 3	435	35	20	18	10	60	835	2 starch, 2 med. fat meat, 3 fat
Chef Salad	1 order	180	5	17	11	0	120	610	1 vegetable, 2 med. fat meat
Chicken Salad w/out Salad Dressing	1 salad	140	8	20	4	tr	50	440	1 vegetable, 2 lean meat

目 = More than 2 fat exchanges per serving   **↑** = More than 800 milligrams sodium   **🛒** = High amounts of sugar

Products	SERVING SIZE	CALORIES	CARBO-HYDRATE (gm)	PROTEIN (gm)	FAT (gm)	SAT. FAT (gm)	CHOLES-TEROL (mg)	SODIUM (mg)	Exchanges
Shrimp and Pasta Salad	1 order	170	14	7	8	tr	0	280	1 starch, 1 lean meat, 1 fat
Onion Rings	1 serving	274	28	4	16	3	0	665	2 starch, 3 fat
French Fries (lightly salted)	Regular	227	24	3	13	7	14	160	1½ starch, 2 fat
Salad Bar (typical) w/out Dressing	1	28	5	2	0	0	0	23	1 vegetable
Garden Salad	1	110	7	6	6	2	10	170	1 vegetable, 1 fat
Salad Dressing	1 pkg.	260-280	5-17	0-2	23-26	3	20	530-690	5 fat
Blue Cheese Salad Dressing	1 pkg.	300	3	2	31	6	40	600	6 fat
Reduced Calorie Italian Salad Dressing	1 pkg.	30	4	0	2	0	0	870	½ fat
Breakfast Croissan'wich	1	304	20	11	19	6	243	637	1½ starch, 1 med. fat meat, 3 fat
Bacon, Egg, Cheese Croissan'wich	1	355	20	14	24	8	249	762	1½ starch, 1 med. fat meat, 4 fat
Sausage, Egg, Cheese Croissan'wich	1	538	20	25	41	14	293	1042	1½ starch, 3 med. fat meat, 5 fat
Ham, Egg, Cheese Croissan'wich	1	335	20	17	20	6	262	987	1½starch, 2 med. fat meat, 2 fat
Scrambled Egg Platter	1	468	33	15	30	*	370	808	2 starch, 1 med. fat meat, 5 fat
Scrambled Egg Platter w/Sausage	1	702	33	24	52	*	420	1213	2 starch, 2 med. fat meat, 8 fat
Scrambled Egg Platter w/Bacon	1	536	33	19	36	*	378	975	2 starch, 2 med. fat meat, 5 fat
French Toast Sticks	1 serving	499	49	9	29	5	74	498	3 starch, ½ med. fat meat, 5 fat
Bagel w/Bacon, Egg, Cheese	1 bagel	438	46	20	19	5	273	905	3 starch, 2 med. fat meat, 1 fat
Bagel w/Ham, Egg, Cheese	1 bagel	418	46	23	15	3	286	1130	3 starch, 2 med. fat meat, 1 fat
Bagel w/Sausage, Egg, Cheese	1 bagel	621	46	26	36	11	317	1185	3 starch, 3 med. fat meat, 4 fat

Products	SERVING SIZE	CALORIES	CARBO-HYDRATE (gm)	PROTEIN (gm)	FAT (gm)	SAT. FAT (gm)	CHOLES-TEROL (mg)	SODIUM (mg)	Exchanges
NOT RECOMMENDED FOR USE									
Vanilla Shake	1	321	49	9	10	*	*	205	
Chocolate Shake	1	320	46	8	12	*	*	202	
Vanilla Shake (syrup added)	1	334	51	9	10	*	*	213	
Chocolate Shake (syrup added)	1	374	60	8	11	*	*	225	
Apple Pie	1	305	44	3	12	4	4	42	
Great Danish	1	500	40	5	36	23	6	288	

CARL'S JR.

Products	SERVING SIZE	CALORIES	CARBO-HYDRATE (gm)	PROTEIN (gm)	FAT (gm)	SAT. FAT (gm)	CHOLES-TEROL (mg)	SODIUM (mg)	Exchanges
Famous Star Hamburger	1 (231 gm.)	590	42	24	36	13	45	890	3 starch, 3 med. fat meat, 3 fat
Super Star Hamburger	1 (301 gm.)	770	44	37	50	21	125	990	3 starch, 4 med. fat meat, 6 fat
Western Bacon Cheeseburger	1 (213 gm.)	630	49	33	33	15	105	1415	3 starch, 4 med. fat meat, 2 fat
Double Western Bacon Cheeseburger	1 (294 gm.)	890	61	42	53	25	145	1620	4 starch, 4 med. fat meat, 6 fat
Old Time Star Hamburger	1 (168 gm.)	400	38	24	17	7	80	760	2½ starch, 3 med. fat meat
Happy Star Hamburger	1 (86 gm.)	220	26	12	8	4	45	445	2 starch, 1 med. fat meat
Charbroiler BBQ Chicken Sandwich	1 (178 gm.)	320	40	28	5	2	50	955	2½ starch, 3 lean meat
Charbroiler Chicken Club Sandwich	1 (234 gm.)	510	53	26	22	2	85	1165	3½ starch, 3 med. fat meat, 1 fat
California Roast Beef 'n Swiss	1 (209 gm.)	360	43	31	8	4	130	1070	3 starch, 3 lean meat
Filet of Fish Sandwich	1 (223 gm.)	550	58	22	26	11	90	945	4 starch, 2 med. fat meat, 3 fat

目 = More than 2 fat exchanges per serving   **ᛏ** = More than 800 milligrams sodium   **🛒** = High amounts of sugar

Products	SERVING SIZE	CALORIES	CARBO-HYDRATE (gm)	PROTEIN (gm)	FAT (gm)	SAT. FAT (gm)	CHOLES-TEROL (mg)	SODIUM (mg)	Exchanges
Chicken Fried Steak Sandwich	1 (205 gm.)	610	54	25	33	12	45	1290	3½ starch, 3 med. fat meat, 3 fat
Hot Dog w/Chili	1 (174 gm.)	510	49	23	25	11	75	1330	3 starch, 2 med. fat meat, 3 fat
American Cheese	1 slice (18 gm.)	63	1	4	5	3	16	290	1 med. fat meat
Swiss Cheese	1 slice (18 gm.)	57	1	4	4	3	16	221	1 lean meat
Fiesta Potato	1 (432 gm.)	550	60	25	23	9	40	1230	4 starch, 2 med. fat meat, 2 fat
Broccoli & Cheese Potato	1 (398 gm.)	470	61	15	17	5	10	690	4 starch, 1 med. fat meat, 2 fat
Bacon & Cheese Potato	1 (400 gm.)	650	63	23	34	12	45	1820	4 starch, 2 med. fat meat, 4 fat
Sour Cream & Chive Potato	1 (294 gm.)	350	49	8	13	5	10	140	3 starch, 3 fat
Cheese Potato	1 (403 gm.)	550	72	18	22	7	40	785	5 starch, 1 med. fat meat, 2 fat
Lite Potato	1 (278 gm.)	250	54	8	tr	0	0	35	3½ starch
French Fries (regular size)	1 order (170 gm.)	360	43	8	17	11	15	626	3 starch, 3 fat
Zucchini	1 order (121 gm.)	300	33	5	16	7	10	480	2 starch, 3 fat
Onion Rings	1 order (90 gm.)	310	38	4	15	7	10	260	2½ starch, 3 fat
Reduced-Cal Italian Dressing	2 oz. (57 gm.)	80	0	0	10	4	0	360	2 fat
House Dressing	2 oz. (57 gm.)	186	6	1	17	2	7	329	4 fat
Blue Cheese Dressing	2 oz. (57 gm.)	150	3	3	14	2	8	278	3 fat
1000 Island Dressing	2 oz. (57 gm.)	231	7	0	23	3	0	435	5 fat
Orange Juice	Small (249 gm.)	94	21	2	1	0	0	2	1½ fruit

Products	SERVING SIZE	CALORIES	CARBO-HYDRATE (gm)	PROTEIN (gm)	FAT (gm)	SAT. FAT (gm)	CHOLES-TEROL (mg)	SODIUM (mg)	Exchanges
Soups: Cream of Broccoli	1 order (186 gm.)	140	14	7	6	4	22	845	1 starch, 1 med. fat meat
Boston Clam Chowder	1 order (186 gm.)	140	12	6	8	3	22	861	1 starch, 1 med. fat meat
Old Fashioned Chicken Noodle	1 order (186 gm.)	80	11	4	1	tr	14	605	1 starch
Lumber Jack Mix Vegetable	1 order (186 gm.)	70	10	2	3	tr	3	807	1 starch
Sunrise Sandwich w/Bacon	1 (127 gm.)	370	32	17	19	8	120	750	2 starch, 2 med. fat meat, 2 fat
Sunrise Sandwich w/Sausage	1 (174 gm.)	500	31	22	32	12	165	990	2 starch, 2½ med. fat meat, 4 fat
French Toast Dips (syrup not included)	1 order (132 gm.)	480	54	8	25	10	54	576	3½ starch, 5 fat
Scrambled Eggs	1 order (67 gm.)	120	2	9	9	4	245	105	1 med. fat meat, 1 fat
Hot Cakes w/Margarine (syrup not included)	1 order (156 gm.)	360	59	7	12	3	15	1190	4 starch, 2 fat
English Muffin w/Margarine	1 (57 gm.)	180	28	4	6	2	0	275	2 starch, 1 fat
Sausage	1 patty (44 gm.)	190	1	7	17	4	25	275	1 high fat meat, 2 fat
Bacon	2 strips (10 gm.)	50	0	3	4	3	8	200	1 fat
Hashed Brown Nuggets	1 order (85 gm.)	170	20	2	9	4	10	350	1 starch, 2 fat
Blueberry Muffins	1 (99 gm.)	256	40	4	7	1	34	360	3 starch, 1 fat
Bran Muffins	1 (113 gm.)	220	34	4	6	0	50	300	2 starch, 1 fat

OCCASIONAL USE

Products	SERVING SIZE	CALORIES	CARBO-HYDRATE (gm)	PROTEIN (gm)	FAT (gm)	SAT. FAT (gm)	CHOLES-TEROL (mg)	SODIUM (mg)	Exchanges
Danish (varieties)	1 (99 gm.)	300	49	8	9	3	0	550	3 starch, 2 fat

▉ = More than 2 fat exchanges per serving   ⊥ = More than 800 milligrams sodium   ♥ = High amounts of sugar

Products	SERVING SIZE	CALORIES	CARBO-HYDRATE (gm)	PROTEIN (gm)	FAT (gm)	SAT. FAT (gm)	CHOLES-TEROL (mg)	SODIUM (mg)	Exchanges
♥ Chocolate Chip Cookies	1 order (64 gm.)	330	44	3	13	1	0	285	3 starch, 2 fat

NOT RECOMMENDED FOR USE

Products	SERVING SIZE	CALORIES	CARBO-HYDRATE (gm)	PROTEIN (gm)	FAT (gm)	SAT. FAT (gm)	CHOLES-TEROL (mg)	SODIUM (mg)	Exchanges
♥ 8 Chocolate Cake	1 order (92 gm.)	380	43	7	20	6	70	335	
♥ Shakes	Reg. size (330 gm.)	353	61	11	7	4	17	255	

CHICK-FIL-A

Products	SERVING SIZE	CALORIES	CARBO-HYDRATE (gm)	PROTEIN (gm)	FAT (gm)	SAT. FAT (gm)	CHOLES-TEROL (mg)	SODIUM (mg)	Exchanges
Chick-Fil-A (no bun)	1 (3.6 oz.)	219	2	36	7	*	42	552	5 lean meat
ⵏ Chick-Fil-A Sandwich (w/bun)	1 (5.8 oz.)	426	40	42	9	*	66	1174	2½ starch, 5 lean meat
ⵏ Chick-Fil-A Nuggets	8-pack (4 oz.)	287	13	28	15	*	61	1326	1 starch, 3 med. fat meat
ⵏ Chick-Fil-A Nuggets	12-pack (6 oz.)	430	19	42	23	*	92	1989	1 starch, 5 med. fat meat
Hearty Breast of Chicken Soup	small (8.5 oz.)	152	11	16	3	*	46	530	1 starch, 2 lean meat
ⵏ Hearty Breast of Chicken Soup	medium (14 oz.)	230	19	27	5	*	80	890	1 starch, 3 lean meat
ⵏ Hearty Breast of Chicken Soup	large (17.5 oz.)	432	36	52	9	*	92	1746	2 starch, 5 lean meat
8 ⵏ Chicken Salad Sandwich (wheat)	1 (5.7 oz.)	449	35	10	26	*	50	888	2 starch, 1 med. fat meat, 4 fat
8 ⵏ Chicken Salad Plate	1 (11.8 oz.)	875	60	29	63	*	97	1839	4 starch, 3 med. fat meat, 9 fat
8 Chicken Salad Cup	1 (4 oz.)	309	4	12	28	*	21	543	2 med. fat meat, 3½ fat
8 Cole Slaw	1 cup	175	11	1	14	*	13	158	2 vegetable, 3 fat
8 Potato Salad	1 cup	198	14	3	15	*	6	337	1 starch, 3 fat
Carrot-Raisin Salad	1 cup	116	18	1	5	*	6	8	1 fruit, 1 vegetable, 1 fat
8 Waffle, Potato Fries	Regular (3 oz.)	270	33	3	14	*	8	45	2 starch, 3 fat

Products	SERVING SIZE	CALORIES	CARBO-HYDRATE (gm)	PROTEIN (gm)	FAT (gm)	SAT. FAT (gm)	CHOLES-TEROL (mg)	SODIUM (mg)	Exchanges
Iced Tea (unsweetened)	9 fl oz.	3	0	tr	tr	*	0	0	free
Orange Juice	6 fl. oz.	82	20	1	tr	*	0	2	1 fruit

OCCASIONAL USE

Icedream	4.5 oz.	134	19	4	5	*	24	51	1 starch, 1 fat

NOT RECOMMENDED FOR USE

Lemon Pie	1 slice	329	64	8	5	*	7	300	
Fudge Brownies w/Nuts	1 (2.8 oz.)	369	45	5	19	*	tr	212	
Lemonade	Regular (10 fl. oz.)	124	32	tr	tr	*	tr	tr	

CHURCH'S FRIED CHICKEN

Fried Chicken Breast	1 (4.3 oz.)	278	9	21	17	*	*	560	½ starch, 3 med. fat meat
Wing, Breast	1 (4.8 oz.)	303	9	22	20	*	*	583	½ starch, 3 med. fat meat, 1 fat
Thigh	1 (4.2 oz.)	306	9	19	22	*	*	448	½ starch, 3 med. fat meat, 1 fat
Leg	1 (2.9 oz.)	147	5	13	9	*	*	286	2 med. fat meat
Hushpuppy	2	156	23	3	6	*	*	110	1½ starch, 1 fat
Corn w/Butter Oil	1 ear	237	33	4	9	*	*	20	2 starch, 2 fat
French Fries	Regular (85 gm.)	138	20	2	6	*	*	126	1 starch, 1 fat
Hot Dog w/Chili	1	320	23	13	20	*	*	985	1½ starch, 1 med. fat meat, 2 fat
Hot Dog w/Cheese	1	330	21	15	21	*	*	990	1½ starch, 1 med. fat meat, 3 fat
Super Hot Dog	1	520	44	17	27	*	*	1365	3 starch, 1 med. fat meat, 4 fat
Super Hot Dog w/Chili	1	570	47	21	32	*	*	1595	3 starch, 2 med. fat meat, 4 fat
Super Hot Dog w/Cheese	1	580	45	22	34	*	*	1605	3 starch, 2 med. fat meat, 4 fat

◫ = More than 2 fat exchanges per serving   ⵣ = More than 800 milligrams sodium   🛒 = High amounts of sugar

Products	SERVING SIZE	CALORIES	CARBO-HYDRATE (gm)	PROTEIN (gm)	FAT (gm)	SAT. FAT (gm)	CHOLES-TEROL (mg)	SODIUM (mg)	Exchanges
Fish Fillet	1	430	45	20	18	*	*	675	3 starch, 2 med. fat meat, 1 fat
Fish Fillet w/Cheese	1	483	46	23	22	*	*	870	3 starch, 2 med. fat meat, 2 fat
Chicken Breast Fillet	1	608	46	27	34	*	*	725	3 starch, 3 med. fat meat, 3 fat
Chicken Breast Fillet w/Cheese	1	661	47	30	38	*	*	921	3 starch, 3 med. fat meat, 4 fat
French Fries	Regular	200	25	2	10	*	*	115	1½ starch, 2 fat
French Fries	Large	320	40	3	16	*	*	185	3 starch, 3 fat
Onion Rings	1 order	280	31	4	16	*	*	140	2 starch, 3 fat
OCCASIONAL USE									
Frozen Dessert	4 oz.	180	27	4	6	*	*	65	2 starch, 1 fat

COLOMBO

Products	SERVING SIZE	CALORIES	CARBO-HYDRATE (gm)	PROTEIN (gm)	FAT (gm)	SAT. FAT (gm)	CHOLES-TEROL (mg)	SODIUM (mg)	Exchanges
Lowfat Frozen Yogurt	4 fl. oz.	99	18	3	2	*	10	35	1 starch, ½ fat
Lite Nonfat Frozen Yogurt	4 fl. oz.	95	21	4	0	*	0	70	1½ starch

D'LITES OF AMERICA

Products	SERVING SIZE	CALORIES	CARBO-HYDRATE (gm)	PROTEIN (gm)	FAT (gm)	SAT. FAT (gm)	CHOLES-TEROL (mg)	SODIUM (mg)	Exchanges
Chicken Fillet Sandwich (on multi-grain bun or white sesame seed bun)	1 (150 gm.)	280	24	23	11	*	*	*	1½ starch, 3 lean meat
Fish Fillet Sandwich (on multi-grain bun or white sesame seed bun)	¼ lb. (167 gm.)	390	29	22	21	*	*	*	2 starch, 2 med. fat meat, 2 fat
Hot Ham 'N Cheese (on multi-grain bun or white sesame seed bun)	1 (137 gm.)	280	26	27	8	*	*	*	1½ starch, 3 lean meat
Vegetarian D'Lite	1 (188 gm.)	270	20	16	14	*	*	*	1 starch, 2 med. fat meat, 1 fat

Products	SERVING SIZE	CALORIES	CARBO-HYDRATE (gm)	PROTEIN (gm)	FAT (gm)	SAT. FAT (gm)	CHOLES-TEROL (mg)	SODIUM (mg)	Exchanges
Jr. D'Lite (on multi-grain bun or white sesame seed bun)	1 (82 gm.)	200	19	15	7	*	*	*	1 starch, 2 lean meat
¼ lb. D'Lite Burger (on multi-grain bun or white sesame seed bun)	1 (119 gm.)	280	19	25	12	*	*	*	1 starch, 3 med. fat meat
Double D'Lite Burger (on multi-grain bun or white sesame seed bun)	1 (190 gm.)	450	19	44	22	*	*	*	1 starch, 6 med. fat meat
Bacon Cheeseburger (on multi-grain bun or white sesame seed bun)	1 (148 gm.)	370	20	32	18	*	*	*	1 starch, 4 med. fat meat
Soup D'Lite	1 (265 gm.)	130	10	14	4	*	*	*	1 starch, 1 lean meat
Cream of Broccoli Soup	1 (236 gm.)	180	21	8	7	*	*	*	1½ starch, 1 fat
Baked Potato (plain)	1 (10 oz.) (217 gm.)	230	50	6	1	*	*	*	3 starch
Baked Potato w/ Broccoli & Cheddar	1 (367 gm.)	410	51	15	16	*	*	*	3 starch, 1 med. fat meat, 2 fat
Baked Potato w/Bacon & Cheddar	1 (329 gm.)	490	52	25	20	*	*	*	3 starch, 2 med. fat meat, 2 fat
Mexican Potato	1 (369 gm.)	510	61	27	18	*	*	*	4 starch, 2 med. fat meat, 1 fat
French Fries	Regular (92 gm.)	260	34	3	12	*	*	*	2 starch, 2 fat
French Fries	Large (114 gm.)	320	42	4	15	*	*	*	3 starch, 3 fat
Potato Skins	Per skin (37 gm.)	90	6	3	6	*	*	*	½ starch, 1 fat

☈ = More than 2 fat exchanges per serving   **⚦** = More than 800 milligrams sodium   **☕** = High amounts of sugar

Products	SERVING SIZE	CALORIES	CARBO-HYDRATE (gm)	PROTEIN (gm)	FAT (gm)	SAT. FAT (gm)	CHOLES-TEROL (mg)	SODIUM (mg)	Exchanges
Mexi Skins	Per skin (37 gm.)	99	6	4	7	*	*	*	½ starch, 1 fat
Salad Bar Platter	1 (286 gm.)	130	9	10	6	*	*	*	2 vegetable or 1 starch, 1 med. fat meat
Reduced Calorie Dressing or Lite Mayonnaise	1 Tbsp.	40	1	tr	4	*	*	*	1 fat
Lite Cheese	1 slice (¾ oz.)	53	2	5	3	*	*	*	1 lean meat
Lite Tartar Sauce	1 Tbsp.	60	2	tr	6	*	*	*	1 fat

OCCASIONAL USE

Products	SERVING SIZE	CALORIES	CARBO-HYDRATE (gm)	PROTEIN (gm)	FAT (gm)	SAT. FAT (gm)	CHOLES-TEROL (mg)	SODIUM (mg)	Exchanges
☗ Chocolate D'Lite	1 (156 gm.)	203	36	6	4	*	*	*	2 starch, 1 fat

DAIRY QUEEN

Products	SERVING SIZE	CALORIES	CARBO-HYDRATE (gm)	PROTEIN (gm)	FAT (gm)	SAT. FAT (gm)	CHOLES-TEROL (mg)	SODIUM (mg)	Exchanges
Single Hamburger	1 (148 gm.)	360	33	21	16	*	45	630	2 starch, 2 med. fat meat, 1 fat
Double Hamburger	1 (210 gm.)	530	33	36	28	*	85	660	2 starch, 4 med. fat meat, 2 fat
Triple Hamburger	1 (272 gm.)	710	33	51	45	*	135	690	2 starch, 6 med. fat meat, 3 fat
Single w/Cheese	1 (162 gm.)	410	33	24	20	*	50	790	2 starch, 3 med. fat meat, 1 fat
Double w/Cheese	1 (239 gm.)	650	34	43	37	*	95	980	2 starch, 5 med. fat meat, 3 fat
Triple w/Cheese	1 (301 gm.)	820	34	58	50	*	145	1010	2 starch, 7 med. fat meat, 3 fat
Hot Dog	1 (100 gm.)	280	21	11	16	*	45	830	1½ starch, 1 med. fat meat, 2 fat
Hot Dog w/Chili	1 (128 gm.)	320	23	13	20	*	55	985	1½ starch, 1 med. fat meat, 2 fat
Hot Dog w/Cheese	1 (114 gm.)	330	21	15	21	*	55	990	1½ starch, 1 med. fat meat, 3 fat
Super Hot Dog	1 (175 gm.)	520	44	17	27	*	80	1365	3 starch, 1 med. fat meat, 4 fat
Super Hot Dog w/Chili	1 (218 gm.)	570	47	21	32	*	100	1595	3 starch, 2 med. fat meat, 4 fat

Products	SERVING SIZE	CALORIES	CARBO-HYDRATE (gm)	PROTEIN (gm)	FAT (gm)	SAT. FAT (gm)	CHOLES-TEROL (mg)	SODIUM (mg)	Exchanges
Super Hot Dog w/Cheese	1 (196 gm.)	580	45	22	34	*	100	1605	3 starch, 2 med. fat meat, 4 fat
Fish Sandwich	1 (170 gm.)	400	41	20	17	*	50	875	3 starch, 2 med. fat meat, 1 fat
Fish Sandwich w/Cheese	1 (177 gm.)	440	39	24	21	*	60	1035	2½ starch, 2 med. fat meat, 2 fat
Chicken Sandwich	1 (220 gm.)	670	46	29	41	*	75	870	3 starch, 3 med. fat meat, 5 fat
Brazier Products: Fish Fillet	1 (177 gm.)	430	45	20	18	*	40	674	3 starch, 2 med. fat meat, 1 fat
Fish Fillet w/Cheese	1 (191 gm.)	483	46	23	22	*	49	870	3 starch, 2 med. fat meat, 2 fat
Chicken Breast Fillet	1 (202 gm.)	608	46	27	34	*	78	725	3 starch, 3 med. fat meat, 3 fat
Chicken Breast Fillet w/Cheese	1 (216 gm.)	661	47	30	38	*	87	921	3 starch, 4 med. fat meat, 3 fat
All White Chicken Nuggets	1 order (99 gm.)	276	13	16	18	*	39	505	1 starch, 2 med. fat meat, 1 fat
BBQ Nugget Sauces	1 pkg. (28 gm.)	41	9	0	0	*	0	130	½ fruit
"DQ" Hounder	1 (151 gm.)	480	21	16	36	*	80	1800	1½ starch, 2 med. fat meat, 5 fat
"DQ" Hounder w/Chili	1 (208 gm.)	575	25	22	41	*	89	1900	2 starch, 2 med. fat meat, 6 fat
"DQ" Hounder w/Cheese	1 (165 gm.)	533	22	19	40	*	89	1995	1½ starch, 2 med. fat meat, 6 fat
French Fries	Regular	200	25	2	10	*	10	115	1½ starch, 2 fat
French Fries	Large	320	40	3	16	*	15	185	3 starch, 3 fat
Onion Rings	1 order (85 gm.)	280	31	4	16	*	15	140	2 starch, 3 fat
Lettuce	14 gm.	2	0	0	0	*	0	10	Free
Tomato	14 gm.	4	1	0	0	*	0	10	Free

🯄 = More than 2 fat exchanges per serving   ⵙ = More than 800 milligrams sodium   ♟ = High amounts of sugar

Products	SERVING SIZE	CALORIES	CARBO-HYDRATE (gm)	PROTEIN (gm)	FAT (gm)	SAT. FAT (gm)	CHOLES-TEROL (mg)	SODIUM (mg)	Exchanges
OCCASIONAL USE									
Frozen Dessert	4 oz.	180	27	4	6	*	15	65	2 starch, 1 fat
Cone	Small	140	22	3	4	*	10	45	1½ starch, 1 fat
Cone	Regular	240	38	6	7	*	15	80	2½ starch, 1 fat
Dipped Cone	Small	190	25	3	9	*	10	55	1½ starch, 2 fat
Mr. Misty Kiss	1	70	17	0	0	*	0	10	1 fruit
Chocolate Sundae	Small	190	33	3	4	*	10	75	2 starch, 1 fat
Mr. Misty	Small	190	48	0	0	*	0	10	3 fruit
DQ Sandwich	1	140	24	3	4	*	5	40	1½ starch, 1 fat
Dilly Bar	1	210	21	3	13	*	10	50	1½ starch, 2 fat
NOT RECOMMENDED FOR USE									
Queen's Choice Vanilla Cone	1	322	40	4	16	*	52	71	
Queen's Choice Chocolate Cone	1	326	40	5	16	*	52	84	
Chipper Sandwich	1	318	56	5	7	*	13	170	
Cone	Large	340	57	9	10	*	25	110	
Dipped Cone	Regular	340	42	6	16	*	20	100	
Dipped Cone	Large	570	64	9	24	*	30	145	
Chocolate Sundae	Regular	310	56	5	8	*	20	120	
Chocolate Sundae	Large	440	78	8	10	*	30	165	
Chocolate Malt	Small	520	91	10	13	*	35	180	
Chocolate Malt	Regular	760	134	14	18	*	50	260	
Chocolate Malt	Large	1060	187	20	25	*	70	360	
Float	1	410	82	5	7	*	20	85	
Hot Fudge Brownie Delight	1	600	85	9	25	*	20	225	
Buster Bar	1	460	41	10	29	*	10	175	

Products	SERVING SIZE	CALORIES	CARBO- HYDRATE (gm)	PROTEIN (gm)	FAT (gm)	SAT. FAT (gm)	CHOLES- TEROL (mg)	SODIUM (mg)	Exchanges
Chocolate Shake	Small	490	82	10	13	*	35	180	
Chocolate Shake	Regular	710	120	14	19	*	50	260	
Chocolate Shake	Large	990	168	19	26	*	70	360	
Banana Split	1	540	103	9	11	*	30	150	
Parfait	1	430	76	8	8	*	30	140	
Peanut Buster Parfait	1	740	94	16	34	*	30	250	
Double Delight	1	490	69	9	20	*	25	150	
Strawberry Shortcake	1	540	100	10	11	*	25	215	
Freeze	1	500	89	9	12	*	30	180	
Mr. Misty	Regular	250	63	tr	tr	*	0	10	
Mr. Misty	Large	340	84	tr	tr	*	0	10	
Mr. Misty Freeze	1	500	91	9	12	*	30	140	
Mr. Misty Float	1	390	74	5	7	*	20	95	
Fudge Nut Bar	1	406	40	8	25	*	10	167	
Heath Blizzard	1	800	125	15	24	*	65	325	
Queen Malt	Large (21 oz.)	889	157	16	21	*	60	304	
Queen Shake	Large (21 oz.)	831	140	16	22	*	60	304	
Queen's Choice Cone	1	325	40	4	16	*	52	75	

DOMINO'S PIZZA

| Cheese Pizza 16" (large) | 2 slices (5.5 oz.) | 376 | 56 | 22 | 10 | 6 | 19 | 483 | 4 starch, 2 med. fat meat |

⯐ = More than 2 fat exchanges per serving   **⍙** = More than 800 milligrams sodium   **🛒** = High amounts of sugar

Products	SERVING SIZE	CALORIES	CARBO-HYDRATE (gm)	PROTEIN (gm)	FAT (gm)	SAT. FAT (gm)	CHOLES-TEROL (mg)	SODIUM (mg)	Exchanges
✶ Pepperoni Pizza 16" (large)	2 slices (5.5 oz.)	460	56	24	18	9	28	825	4 starch, 2 med. fat meat, 2 fat
Sausage/Mushroom Pizza 16" (large)	2 slices (5.5 oz.)	430	55	24	16	8	28	552	4 starch, 2 med. fat meat, 1 fat
✶ Veggie Pizza 16" (large) includes mushrooms, onion, green pepper, double cheese, olives	2 slices (5.5 oz.)	498	60	31	19	10	36	1035	4 starch, 3 med. fat meat, 1 fat
✶ Deluxe Pizza 16" (large) includes sausage, pepperoni, onion, green pepper, mushrooms	2 slices (5.5 oz.)	498	59	27	20	9	40	954	4 starch, 2 med. fat meat, 2 fat
✶ Double Cheese/ Pepperoni Pizza 16" (large)	2 slices (5.5 oz.)	545	55	32	25	13	48	1042	4 starch, 3 med. fat meat, 2 fat
✶ Ham Pizza 16" (large)	2 slices (5.5 oz.)	417	58	23	11	6	26	805	4 starch, 2 med. fat meat

GODFATHER'S PIZZA

Products	SERVING SIZE	CALORIES	CARBO-HYDRATE (gm)	PROTEIN (gm)	FAT (gm)	SAT. FAT (gm)	CHOLES-TEROL (mg)	SODIUM (mg)	Exchanges
Original Pizza: Cheese Pizza — mini	¼ of whole (79 gm.)	190	31	8	4	*	8	260	2 starch, ½ med. fat meat
Cheese Pizza — small	1/6 of whole (101 gm.)	240	32	12	7	*	15	400	2 starch, 1 med. fat meat
Cheese Pizza — medium	⅛ of whole (112 gm.)	270	36	13	8	*	15	430	2 starch, 1½ med. fat meat
Cheese Pizza — large, Hot Slice	⅛ of whole (156 gm.)	370	48	18	11	*	25	620	3 starch, 2 med. fat meat
Cheese Pizza — large	1/10 of whole (125 gm.)	297	39	15	9	*	20	494	2½ starch, 1½ med. fat meat
Combo Pizza — mini	¼ of whole (108 gm.)	240	32	10	7	*	10	450	2 starch, 1 med. fat meat

Products	SERVING SIZE	CALORIES	CARBO-HYDRATE (gm)	PROTEIN (gm)	FAT (gm)	SAT. FAT (gm)	CHOLES-TEROL (mg)	SODIUM (mg)	Exchanges
Combo Pizza — small	1/6 of whole (158 gm.)	360	35	18	15	*	30	830	2 starch, 2 med. fat meat, 1 fat
Combo Pizza — medium	1/8 of whole (175 gm.)	400	39	20	17	*	35	930	2½ starch, 2 med. fat meat, 1 fat
Combo Pizza — large, Hot Slice	1/8 of whole (241 gm.)	550	52	27	24	*	45	1270	3½ starch, 3 med. fat meat, 1 fat
Combo Pizza — large	1/10 of whole (192 gm.)	437	42	22	19	*	36	1019	3 starch, 2 med. fat meat, 1 fat
Thin Crust: Cheese Pizza — small	1/6 of whole (75 gm.)	180	21	9	6	*	10	370	1½ starch, 1 med. fat meat
Cheese Pizza — medium	1/8 of whole (86 gm.)	210	26	10	7	*	14	410	2 starch, 1 med. fat meat
Cheese Pizza — large	1/10 of whole (96 gm.)	228	28	11	7	*	16	464	2 starch, 1 med. fat meat
Combo Pizza — small	1/6 of whole (122 gm.)	270	23	13	13	*	25	710	1½ starch, 1½ med. fat meat, 1 fat
Combo Pizza — medium	1/8 of whole (138 gm.)	310	29	15	14	*	25	790	2 starch, 1½ med. fat meat, 1 fat
Combo Pizza — large	1/10 of whole (152 gm.)	336	31	17	16	*	27	870	2 starch, 2 med. fat meat, 1 fat
Stuffed Pie: Cheese Pizza — small	1/6 of whole (124 gm.)	310	38	13	11	*	25	560	2½ starch, 1 med. fat meat, 1 fat
Cheese Pizza — medium	1/8 of whole (136 gm.)	350	42	14	13	*	25	610	3 starch, 1 med. fat meat, 1 fat

∄ = More than 2 fat exchanges per serving   **⚓** = More than 800 milligrams sodium   **🛒** = High amounts of sugar

Products	SERVING SIZE	CALORIES	CARBO-HYDRATE (gm)	PROTEIN (gm)	FAT (gm)	SAT. FAT (gm)	CHOLES-TEROL (mg)	SODIUM (mg)	Exchanges
Cheese Pizza — large	1/10 of whole (148 gm.)	381	44	16	16	*	32	677	3 starch, 1½ med. fat meat, 1 fat
Combo Pizza — small	1/6 of whole (180 gm.)	430	41	19	20	*	40	1000	3 starch, 2 med. fat meat, 1 fat
Combo Pizza — medium	⅛ of whole (198 gm.)	480	45	21	23	*	43	1105	3 starch, 2 med. fat meat, 2 fat
Combo Pizza — large	1/10 of whole (216 gm.)	521	47	23	26	*	48	1204	3 starch, 2½ med. fat meat, 2½ fat

GOLDEN CORRAL

Products	SERVING SIZE	CALORIES	CARBO-HYDRATE (gm)	PROTEIN (gm)	FAT (gm)	SAT. FAT (gm)	CHOLES-TEROL (mg)	SODIUM (mg)	Exchanges
Sirloin	5-oz. (104 gm.)	230	0	27	14	*	85	270	4 lean meat
Ribeye	Regular (146 gm.)	450	0	34	35	*	120	220	5 med fat meat, 2 fat
Sirloin Tips w/Onions & Peppers	1 order (233 gm.)	290	8	30	13	*	120	260	1 vegetable, 4 lean meat
Chopped Sirloin	Regular (115 gm.)	320	0	28	23	*	100	160	4 med fat meat, 1 fat
Golden Grilled Chicken	1 order (118 gm.)	170	0	32	5	*	100	520	4 lean meat
Golden Fried Chicken Fillets	1 order (155 gm.)	370	14	37	19	*	85	570	1 starch, 5 med. fat meat
Golden Fried Shrimp	1 order (87 gm.)	250	24	12	12	*	90	470	1½ starch, 1 med. fat meat, 1 fat
Baked Potato	1 (219 gm.)	220	46	5	2	*	0	60	3 starch
Texas Toast	1 order (49 gm.)	170	26	5	6	*	0	230	2 starch, 1 fat

HARDEE'S

Products	SERVING SIZE	CALORIES	CARBO-HYDRATE (gm)	PROTEIN (gm)	FAT (gm)	SAT. FAT (gm)	CHOLES-TEROL (mg)	SODIUM (mg)	Exchanges
Hamburger	1 (99 gm.)	264	39	6	10	4	25	500	2½ starch, 1 med. fat meat, 1 fat
Cheeseburger	1 (110 gm.)	310	32	17	13	6	28	681	2 starch, 1½ med. fat meat, 1 fat

Products	SERVING SIZE	CALORIES	CARBO-HYDRATE (gm)	PROTEIN (gm)	FAT (gm)	SAT. FAT (gm)	CHOLES-TEROL (mg)	SODIUM (mg)	Exchanges
¼ lb. Cheeseburger	1 (183 gm.)	510	29	32	29	14	60	1076	2 starch, 2½ med. fat meat, 3 fat
Big Deluxe	1 (226 gm.)	495	33	27	27	12	58	824	2 starch, 3 med. fat meat, 3 fat
Bacon Cheeseburger	1 (229 gm.)	610	33	32	39	16	60	973	2 starch, 4 med. fat meat, 3 fat
Mushroom 'N Swiss	1 (197 gm.)	516	36	29	28	13	55	1031	2½ starch, 3 med. fat meat, 2 fat
Roast Beef Sandwich	1 (141 gm.)	338	31	20	15	6	34	966	2 starch, 2 med. fat meat, 1 fat
Big Roast Beef Sandwich	1 (174 gm.)	396	31	27	18	8	52	1277	2 starch, 3 med. fat meat
Hot Ham 'N Cheese	1 (140 gm.)	316	34	21	10	4	42	1497	2 starch, 2 med. fat meat
Fisherman's Fillet	1 (205 gm.)	510	44	27	25	7	40	861	3 starch, 2½ med. fat meat, 2 fat
Turkey Club	1 (224 gm.)	374	33	28	14	4	45	1296	2 starch, 3 med. fat meat
Chicken Fillet	1 (183 gm.)	416	47	24	16	2	61	1384	3 starch, 2½ med. fat meat
Hot Dog	1 (120 gm.)	306	28	12	16	7	23	776	2 starch, 1 high fat meat, 1 fat
Chicken Stix	6 pieces (100 gm.)	210	13	19	9	2	35	678	1 starch, 2 med fat meat
Chicken Stix	9 pieces (150 gm.)	315	20	28	14	3	53	1017	1 starch, 3 med. fat meat
Garden Salad	1 salad (241 gm.)	208	3	14	14	8	103	266	1 vegetable, 2 med. fat meat, 1 fat
Side Salad	1 (112 gm.)	19	2	2	1	tr	0	14	1 vegetable
Chef Salad	1 (294 gm.)	248	1	28	15	9	114	932	4 lean meat, 1 fat
Chicken Fiesta Salad	1 (297 gm.)	286	6	24	14	9	128	533	1 vegetable, 3 med. fat meat
Regular French Fries	1 (2.5 oz.)	226	30	3	10	2	0	83	2 starch, 2 fat

▌ = More than 2 fat exchanges per serving   ▼ = More than 800 milligrams sodium   🛒 = High amounts of sugar

Products	SERVING SIZE	CALORIES	CARBO-HYDRATE (gm)	PROTEIN (gm)	FAT (gm)	SAT. FAT (gm)	CHOLES-TEROL (mg)	SODIUM (mg)	Exchanges
Large French Fries	1 (4 oz.)	361	48	4	17	3	0	133	3 starch, 3 fat
Hash Rounds Potatoes	1 serving (79 gm.)	232	24	3	14	3	0	558	1½ starch, 3 fat
Rise 'N Shine Biscuit	1 (84 gm.)	319	34	5	19	4	0	722	2 starch, 4 fat
Sausage Biscuit	1 (114 gm.)	448	35	12	30	9	19	1053	2 starch, 1 high fat meat, 4 fat
Sausage & Egg Biscuit	1 (150 gm.)	530	33	16	37	11	141	1123	2 starch, 2 med. fat meat, 5 fat
Bacon Biscuit	1 (84 gm.)	315	34	7	24	7	89	983	2 starch, 4 fat
Bacon & Egg Biscuit	1 (136 gm.)	449	43	15	24	7	89	983	3 starch, 1 med. fat meat, 3 fat
Bacon, Egg, Cheese Biscuit	1 (149 gm.)	492	47	17	27	9	125	1048	3 starch, 1 med. fat meat, 4 fat
Steak Biscuit	1 (150 gm.)	521	48	14	30	6	18	1376	3 starch, 1 med. fat meat, 5 fat
Steak, Egg Biscuit	1 (171 gm.)	563	42	22	34	10	103	1425	3 starch, 2 med. fat meat, 5 fat
Chicken Biscuit	1 (152 gm.)	447	41	15	25	5	9	1308	3 starch, 1 med. fat meat, 4 fat
Ham Biscuit	1 (115 gm.)	321	34	12	15	4	11	1075	2 starch, 1 med. fat meat, 2 fat
Ham, Egg Biscuit	1 (155 gm.)	404	34	17	22	5	159	1132	2 starch, 1½ med. fat meat, 3 fat
Ham, Egg, Cheese Biscuit	1 (171 gm.)	455	38	20	25	7	148	1418	2½ starch, 2 med. fat meat, 3 fat
Country Ham Biscuit	1 (103 gm.)	348	35	12	18	3	17	1282	2 starch, 1 med. fat meat, 3 fat
Country Ham, Egg Biscuit	1 (134 gm.)	404	37	16	22	6	106	1435	2½ starch, 1 med. fat meat, 3 fat
Cinnamon 'N' Raisin Biscuit	1 (79 gm.)	315	37	4	17	5	0	515	2½ starch, 3 fat
Canadian Rise 'N Shine Biscuit	1 (159 gm.)	478	36	20	28	6	187	1550	2 starch, 2 med. fat meat, 4 fat

Products	SERVING SIZE	CALORIES	CARBO-HYDRATE (gm)	PROTEIN (gm)	FAT (gm)	SAT. FAT (gm)	CHOLES-TEROL (mg)	SODIUM (mg)	Exchanges
Biscuit 'N' Gravy	1 (210 gm.)	420	48	9	22	3	10	1379	3 starch, 4 fat
Big Country Breakfast Bacon	1 (240 gm.)	754	45	23	54	9	350	1661	3 starch, 3 med. fat meat, 7 fat
Big Country Breakfast Ham	1 (284 gm.)	768	58	28	47	12	265	2021	4 starch, 3 med. fat meat, 5 fat
Big Country Breakfast Sausage	1 (313 gm.)	1005	55	32	74	16	280	1950	3½ starch, 4 med. fat meat, 10 fat
Orange Juice	6 oz.	83	20	1	tr	tr	0	5	1 fruit

OCCASIONAL USE

Products	SERVING SIZE	CALORIES	CARBO-HYDRATE (gm)	PROTEIN (gm)	FAT (gm)	SAT. FAT (gm)	CHOLES-TEROL (mg)	SODIUM (mg)	Exchanges
Apple Turnover	1 (91 gm.)	268	38	3	12	4	0	245	2 starch, 2 fat
Big Cookie Treat	1 (138 gm.)	250	31	3	13	4	0	239	2 starch, 2 fat
Cool Twist Cone Chocolate	1 (138 gm.)	208	32	6	6	4	18	82	2 starch, 1 fat
Cool Twist Cone Vanilla	1 (124 gm.)	192	30	5	6	4	18	89	2 starch, 1 fat

NOT RECOMMENDED FOR USE

Products	SERVING SIZE	CALORIES	CARBO-HYDRATE (gm)	PROTEIN (gm)	FAT (gm)	SAT. FAT (gm)	CHOLES-TEROL (mg)	SODIUM (mg)	Exchanges
Shake (Chocolate)	1 (335 gm.)	447	83	11	8	5	25	338	

JACK IN THE BOX

Products	SERVING SIZE	CALORIES	CARBO-HYDRATE (gm)	PROTEIN (gm)	FAT (gm)	SAT. FAT (gm)	CHOLES-TEROL (mg)	SODIUM (mg)	Exchanges
Hamburger	1 (103 gm.)	288	29	13	13	5	26	556	2 starch, 1 med. fat meat, 1 fat
Cheeseburger	1 (113 gm.)	325	28	15	17	8	41	746	2 starch, 1½ med. fat meat, 2 fat
Jumbo Jack	1 (222 gm.)	584	42	26	34	11	73	733	3 starch, 3 med. fat meat, 3 fat
Jumbo Jack w/Cheese	1 (242 gm.)	667	46	32	40	14	102	1090	3 starch, 3½ med. fat meat, 4 fat
Bacon Cheeseburger	1 (230 gm.)	705	48	35	39	15	85	1127	3 starch, 3 med. fat meat, 4 fat
Swiss and Bacon Burger	1 (187 gm.)	678	34	31	47	20	92	1458	2 starch, 3½ med. fat meat, 6 fat

〒 = More than 2 fat exchanges per serving   ⟁ = More than 800 milligrams sodium   🛒 = High amounts of sugar

Products	SERVING SIZE	CALORIES	CARBO-HYDRATE (gm)	PROTEIN (gm)	FAT (gm)	SAT. FAT (gm)	CHOLES-TEROL (mg)	SODIUM (mg)	Exchanges
Ultimate Cheeseburger	1 (280 gm.)	942	33	47	69	26	127	1176	2 starch, 6 med. fat meat, 8 fat
Club Pita w/out sauces	1 (179 gm.)	277	28	23	8	4	43	931	2 starch, 2 lean meat
Chicken Supreme	1 (231 gm.)	575	34	27	36	14	62	1525	2 starch, 3 med. fat meat, 4 fat
Pizza Pocket	1 (497 gm.)	497	42	19	28	13	32	940	3 starch, 2 med. fat meat, 3 fat
Moby Jack	1 (137 gm.)	444	39	16	25	8	47	820	2½ starch, 1½ med. fat meat, 3 fat
Fish Supreme	1 (228 gm.)	554	47	20	32	14	30	1047	3 starch, 2 med. fat meat, 4 fat
Hot Club Supreme	1 (213 gm.)	524	38	29	28	9	82	1467	2½ starch, 3 med. fat meat, 3 fat
Sirloin Steak Dinner	1 (334 gm.)	699	75	38	27	10	75	969	5 starch, 3½ med. fat meat, 1 fat
Chicken Strip Dinner	1 (321 gm.)	689	65	40	30	12	100	1213	4 starch, 4 med. fat meat, 2 fat
Shrimp Dinner	1 (301 gm.)	731	77	22	37	17	157	1510	5 starch, 2 med. fat meat, 5 fat
Chef Salad	1 (369 gm.)	295	3	32	78	9	107	812	1 vegetable, 4 med. fat meat
Taco Salad	1 (358 gm.)	377	10	31	24	10	102	1436	½ starch, 4 med. fat meat, 1 fat
Pasta and Seafood Salad	1 (417 gm.)	394	32	15	22	4	48	1570	2 starch, 2 med. fat meat, 2 fat
Side Salad	1 (111 gm.)	51	tr	7	3	2	tr	84	1 lean meat
Dressings: Buttermilk House	1 pkg. (35 gm.)	181	4	tr	18	2.9	10	347	4 fat
Bleu Cheese	1 pkg. (35 gm.)	131	7	tr	11	2	9	459	½ starch, 2 fat
Thousand Island	1 pkg. (35 gm.)	156	6	tr	15	3	11	350	½ starch, 3 fat
Reduced Calorie French	1 pkg. (35 gm.)	80	13	tr	4	1	0	300	½ starch, 1 fat

Products	SERVING SIZE	CALORIES	CARBO-HYDRATE (gm)	PROTEIN (gm)	FAT (gm)	SAT. FAT (gm)	CHOLES-TEROL (mg)	SODIUM (mg)	Exchanges
Taco	1 (81 gm.)	191	16	8	11	5	21	406	1 starch, 1 med. fat meat, 1 fat
Super Taco	1 (135 gm.)	288	21	12	17	8	37	765	1½ starch, 1 med. fat meat, 2 fat
Cheese Nachos	1 (170 gm.)	571	49	15	35	13	37	1154	3 starch, 1 med. fat meat, 6 fat
Supreme Nachos	1 (338)	787	66	29	45	17	59	2194	4 starch, 2 med. fat meat, 7 fat
Fajita Pita	1 (175 gm.)	278	31	19	7	3	30	611	2 starch, 2 lean meat
Guacamole	1 pkg. (25 gm.)	55	2	tr	5	0	0	130	1 fat
Salsa	1 pkg. (25 gm.)	8	2	tr	tr	0	0	129	free
Chicken Fajita Pita	1 (189 gm.)	292	29	24	8	29	34	703	2 starch, 3 lean meat
French Fries	Regular (68 gm.)	221	27	2	12	5	8	164	2 starch, 2 fat
French Fries	Large (109 gm.)	353	43	3	19	8	13	262	3 starch, 3 fat
French Fries	Jumbo (136 gm.)	442	54	4	24	10	16	328	3½ starch, 4 fat
Onion Rings	1 order (108 gm.)	382	39	5	23	11	27	407	2½ starch, 4 fat
Egg Rolls	3 piece (171 gm.)	405	42	15	19	7	30	903	3 starch, 1 med. fat meat, 2 fat
Egg Rolls	5 piece (285 gm.)	675	70	26	32	12	50	1505	5 starch, 2 med. fat meat, 4 fat
Chicken Strips	4 piece (125 gm.)	349	28	29	14	7	68	748	2 starch, 3 med. fat meat
Chicken Strips	6 piece (187 gm.)	523	42	43	20	10	103	1122	3 starch, 5 med. fat meat
Shrimp	10 piece (84 gm.)	270	22	10	16	7	84	669	1½ starch, 1 med. fat meat, 2 fat
Shrimp	15 piece (125 gm.)	404	34	15	24	11	126	1003	2 starch, 1½ med. fat meat, 3 fat

🖁 = More than 2 fat exchanges per serving   🕴 = More than 800 milligrams sodium   🛒 = High amounts of sugar

Products	SERVING SIZE	CALORIES	CARBO-HYDRATE (gm)	PROTEIN (gm)	FAT (gm)	SAT. FAT (gm)	CHOLES-TEROL (mg)	SODIUM (mg)	Exchanges
Sweet & Sour Sauce	1 pkg. (28 gm.)	40	11	tr	tr	0	tr	160	1 fruit
A-1 Steak Sauce	1 pkg. (50 gm.)	35	9	tr	tr	*	0	809	½ starch
BBQ Sauce	1 pkg. (50 gm.)	78	19	tr	tr	*	0	535	1 starch
Seafood Cocktail Sauce	1 pkg. (50 gm.)	57	12	2	tr	*	0	367	1 starch or 2 vegetable
Orange Juice	6 oz.	80	20	1	0	*	0	0	1 fruit
Supreme Crescent	1 (146 gm.)	547	27	20	40	13	178	1053	2 starch, 2 med. fat meat, 6 fat
Sausage Crescent	1 (156 gm.)	584	28	22	43	16	187	1012	2 starch, 2 med. fat meat, 6 fat
Canadian Crescent	1 (134 gm.)	452	25	19	31	10	226	851	2 starch, 2 med. fat meat, 4 fat
Breakfast Jack	1 (126 gm.)	307	30	18	13	5	203	871	2 starch, 2 med. fat meat, 1 fat
Scrambled Egg Platter	1 (249 gm.)	662	52	24	40	17	354	1188	3½ starch, 2 med. fat meat, 6 fat
Hash Browns	1 (62 gm.)	116	11	2	7	4	3	211	1 starch, 1 fat

NOT RECOMMENDED FOR USE

Products	SERVING SIZE	CALORIES	CARBO-HYDRATE (gm)	PROTEIN (gm)	FAT (gm)	SAT. FAT (gm)	CHOLES-TEROL (mg)	SODIUM (mg)	Exchanges
Mayo-Onion Sauce	1 pkg. (21 gm.)	143	tr	1	15	0	20	140	
Mayo-Mustard Sauce	1 pkg. (21 gm.)	124	tr	2	13	0	10	247	
Hot Apple Turnover	1 (119 gm.)	410	45	4	24	11	15	350	
Cheesecake	1 (99 gm.)	309	29	8	18	9	63	208	
Vanilla Milk Shake	1 (317 gm.)	320	57	10	6	4	25	230	
Chocolate Milk Shake	1 (322 gm.)	330	55	11	7	4	25	270	
Strawberry Milk Shake	1 (328 gm.)	320	55	10	7	4	25	240	

Products	SERVING SIZE	CALORIES	CARBO- HYDRATE (gm)	PROTEIN (gm)	FAT (gm)	SAT. FAT (gm)	CHOLES- TEROL (mg)	SODIUM (mg)	Exchanges
Pancake Platter	1 (231 gm.)	612	87	15	22	9	99	888	

KENTUCKY FRIED CHICKEN

Original Recipe Chicken:

Products	SERVING SIZE	CALORIES	CARBO- HYDRATE (gm)	PROTEIN (gm)	FAT (gm)	SAT. FAT (gm)	CHOLES- TEROL (mg)	SODIUM (mg)	Exchanges
Wing	1 (56 gm.)	181	6	12	12	*	*	387	½ starch, 1½ med. fat meat, 1 fat
Side Breast	1 (95 gm.)	276	10	20	17	*	*	654	½ starch, 3 med. fat meat
Center Breast	1 (107 gm.)	257	8	26	14	*	*	532	½ starch, 3 med. fat meat
Drumstick	1 (58 gm.)	147	4	14	9	*	*	269	2 med. fat meat
Thigh	1 (96 gm.)	278	8	18	19	*	*	517	½ starch, 2 med. fat meat, 2 fat

Extra Crispy Chicken:

Products	SERVING SIZE	CALORIES	CARBO- HYDRATE (gm)	PROTEIN (gm)	FAT (gm)	SAT. FAT (gm)	CHOLES- TEROL (mg)	SODIUM (mg)	Exchanges
Wing	1 (57 gm.)	218	8	12	16	*	*	437	½ starch, 1½ med. fat meat, 2 fat
Side Breast	1 (98 gm.)	354	17	18	24	*	*	797	1 starch, 2 med. fat meat, 3 fat
Center Breast	1 (120 gm.)	353	15	27	21	*	*	842	1 starch, 3 med. fat meat, 1 fat
Drumstick	1 (60 gm.)	173	6	13	11	*	*	346	½ starch, 2 med. fat meat
Thigh	1 (112 gm.)	371	14	20	26	*	*	766	1 starch, 2 med. fat meat, 3 fat
Kentucky Nuggets	6 (96 gm.)	276	13	17	17	*	*	840	1 starch, 2 med. fat meat, 1 fat
Barbeque Sauce	1 oz.	35	7	tr	tr	*	*	450	½ starch or fruit
Sweet & Sour Sauce	1 oz.	58	13	tr	tr	*	*	149	1 starch or fruit
Mustard Sauce	1 oz.	36	6	1	1	*	*	346	½ starch or fruit
Buttermilk Biscuits	1 (75 gm.)	269	32	5	14	*	*	521	2 starch, 3 fat
Mashed Potatoes w/Gravy	1 (86 gm.)	62	10	2	1	*	*	297	1 starch

⯐ = More than 2 fat exchanges per serving   **⯚** = More than 800 milligrams sodium   **🛒** = High amounts of sugar

Products	SERVING SIZE	CALORIES	CARBO-HYDRATE (gm)	PROTEIN (gm)	FAT (gm)	SAT. FAT (gm)	CHOLES-TEROL (mg)	SODIUM (mg)	Exchanges
Mashed Potatoes	1 (80 gm.)	59	12	2	tr	*	*	228	1 starch
Chicken Gravy	1 (78 gm.)	59	4	2	4	*	*	398	1 fat
Kentucky Fries	1 (119 gm.)	268	33	5	13	*	*	81	2 starch, 2½ fat
Corn-on-the-Cob	1 (143 gm.)	176	32	5	3	*	*	21	2 starch
Cole Slaw	1 (79 gm.)	103	12	1	6	*	*	171	2 vegetable or 1 starch, 1 fat
Potato Salad	1 (90 gm.)	141	13	2	9	*	*	396	1 starch, 2 fat
Baked Beans	1 (89 gm.)	105	18	5	1	*	*	387	1 starch

LONG JOHN SILVERS

Products	SERVING SIZE	CALORIES	CARBO-HYDRATE (gm)	PROTEIN (gm)	FAT (gm)	SAT. FAT (gm)	CHOLES-TEROL (mg)	SODIUM (mg)	Exchanges
Fish & Fries	3 pc. Fish	853	64	43	48	*	*	2025	4 starch, 4 med. fat meat, 5 fat
Fish & Fries	2 pc. Fish	651	53	30	36	*	*	1352	3½ starch, 2 med. fat meat, 4 fat
Fish & More w/slaw, 2 hushpuppies	2 pc Fish	978	82	34	58	*	*	2124	5 starch, 3 med. fat meat, 1 vegetable, 7 fat
Fish Dinner w/slaw, 2 hushpuppies, fries	3 pc. Fish	1180	93	47	70	*	*	2797	6 starch, 4 med. fat meat, 1 vegetable, 9 fat
Tender Chicken Plank Dinner w/fries, slaw	3 pc. Chicken	885	72	32	51	*	*	1918	4 starch, 3 med. fat meat, 1 vegetable, 7 fat
Tender Chicken Plank Dinner w/fries, slaw	4 pc. Chicken	1037	82	41	59	*	*	2433	5 starch, 4 med. fat meat, 1 vegetable, 7 fat
Shrimp, Fish, Chicken Dinner w/ fries, slaw, 2 hushpuppies	1 pc. Fish 2 Shrimp 2 pc. Chicken	1022	87	34	60	*	*	2274	5 starch, 3 med. fat meat, 1 vegetable, 8 fat
Fish & Chicken w/ fries, slaw	1 pc. Fish 2 pc. Chicken	935	73	36	55	*	*	2076	4 starch, 3 med. fat meat, 1 vegetable, 8 fat

Products	SERVING SIZE	CALORIES	CARBO-HYDRATE (gm)	PROTEIN (gm)	FAT (gm)	SAT. FAT (gm)	CHOLES-TEROL (mg)	SODIUM (mg)	Exchanges
Seafood Platter w/ fries, slaw, 2 hushpuppies	1 pc. Fish 2 Shrimp 2 Scallops	976	85	29	58	*	*	2161	5 starch, 2 med. fat meat, 1 vegetable, 9 fat
Clam Dinner w/ fries, slaw	1	955	100	22	58	*	*	1543	6 starch, 2 med. fat meat, 1 vegetable, 8 fat
Battered Shrimp Dinner w/ fries, slaw	6 Shrimp	711	60	17	45	*	*	1297	4 starch, 1 med. fat meat, 1 vegetable, 7 fat
Breaded Shrimp Platter w/ fries slaw, 2 hushpuppies	1	962	93	20	57	*	*	2007	6 starch, 1 med. fat meat, 1 vegetable, 9 fat
Shrimp & Fish Dinner w/ fries, slaw, 2 hushpuppies	1 Fish 3 Shrimp	917	80	27	55	*	*	1913	5 starch, 2 med. fat meat, 1 vegetable, 8 fat
Scallop Dinner w/ fries, slaw	1	747	66	17	45	*	*	1579	4 starch, 1 med. fat meat, 1 vegetable 8 fat
Oyster Dinner w/ fries, slaw	6 Oysters	789	78	17	45	*	*	763	5 starch, 1 med. fat meat, 1 vegetable, 8 fat
Baked Fish Dinner w/ slaw, mixed vegetables	Fish w/ sauce	387	19	36	19	*	*	1298	1 starch, 4 med. fat meat
Catfish Fillet Dinner w/ fries, slaw, 2 hushpuppies	1	980	86	32	58	*	*	1716	5 starch, 3 med. fat meat, 1 vegetable, 8 fat
Shrimp Salad w/crackers	1	183	12	27	3	*	*	658	1 starch, 3 lean meat
Seafood Salad w/crackers	1	406	18	18	30	*	*	1021	1 starch, 2 med. fat meat, 4 fat
Combo Salad w/crackers	1	377	17	26	3	*	*	1051	1 starch, 3 med. fat meat, 2 fat
Ocean Chef Salad w/crackers	1	222	9	28	8	*	*	983	1 starch, 3 lean meat
Breaded Fish Sandwich Platter w/ fries, slaw	1	835	84	30	42	*	*	1402	5 starch, 3 med. fat meat, 1 vegetable, 4 fat

= More than 2 fat exchanges per serving   = More than 800 milligrams sodium   = High amounts of sugar

Products	SERVING SIZE	CALORIES	CARBO-HYDRATE (gm)	PROTEIN (gm)	FAT (gm)	SAT. FAT (gm)	CHOLES-TEROL (mg)	SODIUM (mg)	Exchanges
Kitchen Breaded Fish w/ fries, slaw, 2 hushpuppies	3 pc. Fish	940	84	35	52	*	*	1900	5 starch, 1 med. fat meat, 1 vegetable, 6 fat
Kitchen Breaded Fish w/ fries, slaw, 2 hushpuppies	2 pc. Fish	818	76	26	46	*	*	1526	4 starch, 2 med. fat meat, 1 vegetable, 7 fat
Kids Meals: One Fish & Fries	1	449	42	16	24	*	*	679	3 starch, 1 med. fat meat, 3 fat
Two Planks & Fries	1	551	51	22	28	*	*	1036	3 starch, 2 med. fat meat, 3 fat
A La Carte: Battered Fish	1 (3 oz.)	202	11	13	12	*	*	673	1 starch, 1 med. fat meat, 1 fat
Kitchen Breaded Fish	1 (2 oz.)	122	8	9	5	*	*	374	½ starch, 1 med. fat meat
Catfish Fillet	1 (2.7 oz.)	203	13	12	12	*	*	469	1 starch, 1 med. fat meat, 1 fat
Tender Chicken Plank	1 (2.2 oz.)	152	10	9	8	*	*	515	1 starch, 1 med. fat meat
Breaded Clams	1 order (4.7 oz.)	526	48	17	31	*	*	1170	3 starch, 1 med. fat meat, 5 fat
Battered Scallops	3 pc. (2.1 oz.)	159	12	6	9	*	*	503	1 starch, 1 high fat meat
Breaded Oysters	3 pc. (2.1 oz.)	180	18	6	9	*	*	195	1 starch, 1 high fat meat
Battered Shrimp	3 pc. (1.8 oz.)	141	9	6	9	*	*	462	1 starch, 1 high fat meat
Breaded Shrimp	1 order (4.7 oz.)	388	33	12	23	*	*	1229	2 starch, 1 med. fat meat, 3 fat
Seafood Salad	1 (5.6 oz.)	338	6	16	28	*	*	924	2 med. fat meat, 1 vegetable, 3 fat
Baked Fish w/sauce	1 (5.5 oz.)	151	0	33	2	*	*	361	4 lean meat
Breaded Fish	1 (6.6 oz.)	406	42	25	15	*	*	1029	3 starch, 3 med. fat meat

Products	SERVING SIZE	CALORIES	CARBO-HYDRATE (gm)	PROTEIN (gm)	FAT (gm)	SAT. FAT (gm)	CHOLES-TEROL (mg)	SODIUM (mg)	Exchanges
Clam Chowder	1 order (6.6 oz.)	128	15	7	5	*	*	611	1 starch, 1 med. fat meat
Fries	1 order (3 oz.)	247	31	4	12	*	*	6	2 starch, 2 fat
Hushpuppies	2 pc. (1.7 oz.)	145	18	3	7	*	*	405	1 starch, 1½ fat
Corn on the Cob	1 ear	176	29	5	4	*	*	tr	2 starch
Mixed Vegetables	1 order (4 oz.)	54	8	2	2	*	*	270	2 vegetable
Condiments:									
Seafood Sauce	1 oz.	34	9	tr	tr	*	*	357	1 vegetable
Tartar Sauce	1 oz.	117	5	tr	11	*	*	228	2 fat
Bleu Cheese Dressing	1.5 oz.	225	3	2	23	*	*	*	5 fat
1000 Island Dressing	1.5 oz.	225	8	tr	22	*	*	422	5 fat
Reduced Calorie Italian Dressing	1.5 oz.	20	3	tr	1	*	*	882	Free
Sea Salad Dressing	1.5 oz.	220	5	2	21	*	*	*	5 fat

OCCASIONAL USE

Honey Mustard Sauce	1 oz.	56	14	tr	tr	*	*	315	1 fruit
Apple Pie	4 oz.	280	43	2	11	*	*	247	3 starch, 2 fat
Pumpkin Pie	4 oz.	251	34	4	11	*	*	242	2 starch, 2 fat
Cherry Pie	4 oz.	294	46	3	11	*	*	287	3 starch, 2 fat
Lemon Meringue	3.5 oz.	200	37	2	6	*	*	254	2 starch, 1 fat

NOT RECOMMENDED FOR USE

Pecan Pie	4 oz.	446	59	5	22	*	*	435	

MCDONALD'S

Hamburger	1 (102 gm.)	257	31	12	10	4	37	460	2 starch, 1 med. fat meat, 1 fat

= More than 2 fat exchanges per serving
= More than 800 milligrams sodium
= High amounts of sugar

Products	SERVING SIZE	CALORIES	CARBO-HYDRATE (gm)	PROTEIN (gm)	FAT (gm)	SAT. FAT (gm)	CHOLES-TEROL (mg)	SODIUM (mg)	Exchanges
Cheeseburger	1 (114 gm.)	308	31	15	14	5	53	750	2 starch, 1½ med. fat meat, 1 fat
Quarter Pounder	1 (166 gm.)	414	34	23	21	8	86	660	2 starch, 3 med. fat meat, 1 fat
Quarter Pounder w/Cheese	1 (194 gm.)	517	35	29	29	11	118	1150	2 starch, 3½ med. fat meat, 2 fat
Big Mac	1 (215 gm.)	562	43	25	32	10	103	950	3 starch, 3 med. fat meat, 3 fat
Filet-O-Fish	1 (142 gm.)	442	38	14	26	5	50	1030	2½ starch, 1 med. fat meat, 4 fat
McD.L.T.	1 (288 gm.)	674	46	28	42	12	112	1170	3 starch, 3 med. fat meat, 5 fat
Chicken McNuggets	6 (113 gm.)	288	17	19	16	4	65	520	1 starch, 2 med. fat meat, 1 fat
Hot Mustard Sauce	1 (30 gm.)	66	8	tr	4	tr	5	250	1 fruit
Barbeque Sauce	1 (32 gm.)	53	12	tr	tr	0	0	340	1 fruit
Sweet and Sour Sauce	1 (32 gm.)	57	14	tr	tr	0	0	190	1 fruit
French Fries	Regular (68 gm.)	220	26	3	12	5	9	110	2 starch, 2 fat
French Fries	Large (97 gm.)	312	37	4	16	7	12	155	2½ starch, 3 fat
Orange or Grapefruit Juice	6 oz.	80	19	1	0	0	0	0	1 fruit
Chef Salad	1 (283 gm.)	231	8	21	14	6	152	490	1 vegetable, 3 med. fat meat
Shrimp Salad	1 (262 gm.)	104	6	14	3	1	193	480	1 vegetable, 2 lean meat
Garden Salad	1 (213 gm.)	112	6	7	7	3	107	160	1 vegetable, 1 med. fat meat
Chicken Salad Oriental	1 (244 gm.)	141	5	23	3	1	78	230	1 vegetable, 3 lean meat
Side Salad	1 (115 gm.)	57	3	4	3	1	53	85	1 vegetable, ½ fat
Croutons	11 (11 gm.)	52	7	1	2	1	0	140	½ starch

Products	SERVING SIZE	CALORIES	CARBO-HYDRATE (gm)	PROTEIN (gm)	FAT (gm)	SAT. FAT (gm)	CHOLES-TEROL (mg)	SODIUM (mg)	Exchanges
Bacon Bits	1 (3 gm.)	16	tr	1	1	0	0	95	Free
Chow Mein Noodles	1 (9 gm.)	45	5	1	2	1	2	60	½ starch, ½ fat
Dressings: Blue Cheese	.5 oz.	69	1	1	7	1	6	150	1½ fat
French	.5 oz.	58	3	tr	5	1	0	180	1 fat
Ranch	.5 oz.	83	1	tr	9	1	5	130	2 fat
1000 Island	.5 oz.	78	2	tr	8	1	8	100	2 fat
Lite Vinagrette	.5 oz.	15	2	tr	1	tr	0	60	Free
Oriental	.5 oz.	24	6	tr	tr	0	0	180	½ fruit
Egg McMuffin	1 (138 gm.)	293	28	18	12	4	299	740	2 starch, 2 med. fat meat
Scrambled Eggs	1 (100 gm.)	157	1	12	11	3	545	290	2 med. fat meat
Pork Sausage	1 (48 gm.)	180	0	8	16	6	48	350	1 high fat meat, 2 fat
English Muffin w/butter	1 (59 gm.)	169	27	5	5	2	9	270	2 starch, 1 fat
Hash Brown Potatoes	1 (53 gm.)	131	15	2	7	3	9	330	1 starch, 1½ fat
Biscuit w/Biscuit Spread	1 (75 gm.)	260	32	5	13	3	1	730	2 starch, 2½ fat
Biscuit w/Sausage	1 (123 gm.)	440	32	13	29	9	49	1080	2 starch, 1 high fat meat, 4 fat
Biscuit w/Sausage and Egg	1 (180 gm.)	529	33	20	35	11	358	1250	2 starch, 2 med. meat, 5 fat
Biscuit w/Bacon, Egg and Cheese	1 (156 gm.)	449	33	17	27	8	336	1230	2 starch, 2 med. fat meat, 3 fat
Sausage McMuffin	1 (117 gm.)	372	27	17	22	8	64	830	2 starch, 2 med. fat meat, 2 fat
Sausage McMuffin w/Egg	1 (167 gm.)	440	28	23	27	9	263	980	2 starch, 3 med. fat meat, 2 fat

目 = More than 2 fat exchanges per serving　　**▲** = More than 800 milligrams sodium　　**♥** = High amounts of sugar

Products	SERVING SIZE	CALORIES	CARBO-HYDRATE (gm)	PROTEIN (gm)	FAT (gm)	SAT. FAT (gm)	CHOLES-TEROL (mg)	SODIUM (mg)	Exchanges
OCCASIONAL USE									
Apple Pie	1 (83 gm.)	262	30	2	15	5	6	240	2 starch, 3 fat
Soft Serve Cone	1 (86 gm.)	144	22	4	5	2	16	70	1½ starch, 1 fat
NOT RECOMMENDED FOR USE									
Vanilla Shake	1 (303 gm.)	354	56	10	10	5	41	170	
Chocolate Shake	1 (303 gm.)	388	63	11	11	5	41	240	
Strawberry Shake	1 (303 gm.)	384	63	10	10	5	41	170	
Strawberry Sundae	1 (171 gm.)	283	48	6	7	3	27	85	
Hot Fudge Sundae	1 (169 gm.)	313	50	7	9	5	28	160	
Hot Caramel Sundae	1 (174 gm.)	343	58	7	9	4	35	160	
McDonaldland Cookie	1 box (56 gm.)	288	47	4	9	2	0	300	
Chocolate Chip Cookie	1 box (56 gm.)	325	42	4	16	5	4	280	
Hot Cakes w/Butter, Syrup	1 (176 gm.)	413	74	8	9	4	21	640	
Apple Danish	1 (115 gm.)	389	51	6	18	3	25	370	
Hot Cheese Danish	1 (110 gm.)	395	42	7	22	6	47	420	
Cinnamon Raisin Danish	1 (110 gm.)	445	58	6	21	4	34	430	
Raspberry Danish	1 (117 gm.)	414	62	6	16	3	26	310	

MRS. WINNER'S CHICKEN & BISCUITS

Products	SERVING SIZE	CALORIES	CARBO-HYDRATE (gm)	PROTEIN (gm)	FAT (gm)	SAT. FAT (gm)	CHOLES-TEROL (mg)	SODIUM (mg)	Exchanges
Biscuit	1 (66 gm.)	245	45	4	5	*	tr	503	3 starch, 1 fat

Products	Serving Size	Calories	Carbo-hydrate (gm)	Protein (gm)	Fat (gm)	Sat. Fat (gm)	Choles-terol (mg)	Sodium (mg)	Exchanges
Sausage Patties	1 (37 gm.)	200	tr	6	10	*	8	400	1 high fat meat, 1 fat
Country Ham	1 (26 gm.)	60	tr	4	1	*	14	565	1 lean meat
Baked Chicken Fillet	1 (87 gm.)	120	tr	10	2	*	33	360	2 lean meat
Country Fried Steak	1 (62 gm.)	220	tr	12	14	*	7	205	2 high fat meat
Breaded Chicken Sandwich	1 (92 gm.)	203	12	19	10	*	37	1000	1 starch, 2 med. fat meat
Baked Beans	1 order (125 gm.)	149	31	5	tr	*	1	436	2 starch
Cole Slaw	1 order (105 gm.)	188	9	1	16	*	1	549	2 vegetable, 3 fat
Potato Fries	1 order (107 gm.)	225	27	6	9	*	1	214	2 starch, 2 fat
Mashed Potatoes w/Gravy	1 order (174 gm.)	148	22	3	3	*	2	823	1½ starch, 1 fat
Seafood Salad	1 (367 gm.)	553	41	5	9	*	4	756	3 starch, 2 fat
Chicken Salad	1 (389 gm.)	583	39	9	8	*	3	875	3 starch, 2 fat
Chicken Salad Sandwich	1 (184 gm.)	313	33	10	6	*	1	599	2 starch, 2 lean meat
Chicken Fillet Sandwich	1 (180 gm.)	379	45	12	7	*	28	541	3 starch, 2 lean meat
Steak Sandwich	1 (179 gm.)	429	43	11	11	*	21	644	3 starch, 2 med. fat meat
Tossed Salad	1 (115 gm.)	6	1	1	tr	*	1	439	1 vegetable

PIZZA HUT

Products	Serving Size	Calories	Carbo-hydrate (gm)	Protein (gm)	Fat (gm)	Sat. Fat (gm)	Choles-terol (mg)	Sodium (mg)	Exchanges
Thin-n-Crispy Pizza, Beef	3 slices ½ 10" pizza	490	51	29	19	*	*	*	3 starch, 3 med. fat meat, 1 fat

🁢 = More than 2 fat exchanges per serving   🕯 = More than 800 milligrams sodium   🛒 = High amounts of sugar

Products	SERVING SIZE	CALORIES	CARBO-HYDRATE (gm)	PROTEIN (gm)	FAT (gm)	SAT. FAT (gm)	CHOLES-TEROL (mg)	SODIUM (mg)	Exchanges
Thin-n-Crispy Pizza, Pork	3 slices ½ 10" pizza	520	51	27	23	*	*	*	3 starch, 3 med. fat meat, 1 fat
Thin-n-Crispy Pizza, Cheese	3 slices ½ 10" pizza	450	54	25	15	*	*	*	3½ starch, 2 med. fat meat, 1 fat
Thin-n-Crispy Pizza, Pepperoni	3 slices ½ 10" pizza	430	45	23	17	*	*	*	3 starch, 2 med. fat meat, 1 fat
Thin-n-Crispy Pizza, Supreme	3 slices ½ 10" pizza	510	51	27	21	*	*	*	3 starch, 3 med. fat meat, 1 fat
Thick 'n Chewy Pizza, Beef	3 slices ½ 10" pizza	620	73	38	20	*	*	*	5 starch, 4 med. fat meat
Thick 'n Chewy Pizza, Pork	3 slices ½ 10" pizza	640	71	36	23	*	*	*	5 starch, 4 med. fat meat
Thick 'n Chewy Pizza, Cheese	3 slices ½ 10" pizza	560	71	34	14	*	*	*	5 starch, 3 med. fat meat
Thick 'n Chewy Pizza, Pepperoni	3 slices ½ 10" pizza	560	68	31	18	*	*	*	4½ starch, 3 med. fat meat
Thick 'n Chewy Pizza, Supreme	3 slices ½ 10" pizza	640	74	36	22	*	*	*	5 starch, 4 med. fat meat

PONDEROSA

Products	SERVING SIZE	CALORIES	CARBO-HYDRATE (gm)	PROTEIN (gm)	FAT (gm)	SAT. FAT (gm)	CHOLES-TEROL (mg)	SODIUM (mg)	Exchanges
Fish, baked Bake 'R Broil	5.2 oz.	230	10	19	13	*	50	330	1 starch, 2 med. fat meat
Baked Scrod	7.0 oz.	120	0	27	1	*	65	80	3 lean meat
Fish, broiled Halibut	6.0 oz.	170	0	35	3	*	*	68	4 lean meat
Roughy	5.0 oz.	139	*	21	5	*	28	88	3 lean meat
Salmon	6.0 oz.	192	3	37	3	*	60	72	4 lean meat
Swordfish	5.9 oz.	271	0	44	10	*	84	0	5 lean meat
Trout	5.0 oz.	228	1	30	4	*	110	51	4 lean meat

Products	SERVING SIZE	CALORIES	CARBO-HYDRATE (gm)	PROTEIN (gm)	FAT (gm)	SAT. FAT (gm)	CHOLES-TEROL (mg)	SODIUM (mg)	Exchanges
Fish, fried	3.2 oz.	190	17	9	9	*	15	170	1 starch, 1 med. fat meat, 1 fat
Shrimp, fried	7 pieces	230	31	22	1	*	105	612	2 starch, 2 lean meat
Chicken breast	5.5 oz.	98	1	20	2	*	54	400	3 lean meat
Chopped steak	4.0 oz.	225	1	19	16	*	80	150	3 med. fat meat
Chopped steak	5.3 oz.	296	1	25	22	*	105	296	4 med. fat meat
Hot dog	1.6 oz.	144	1	5	13	*	27	460	1 high fat meat, 1 fat
Kansas City strip	5 oz.	138	1	21	6	*	76	850	3 lean meat
New York Strip, Choice	10 oz.	314	1	45	15	*	50	1420	6 lean meat
New York Strip, Choice	8 oz.	304	2	34	11	*	62	570	5 lean meat
Porterhouse, Choice	16 oz.	640	3	57	31	*	82	1130	8 med. fat meat
Porterhouse, Non-graded	13 oz.	440	1	43	30	*	67	1844	6 med. fat meat
Ribeye, Choice	6 oz.	282	1	29	14	*	60	570	4 med. fat meat
Ribeye, Non-graded	5 oz.	219	1	25	13	*	75	1130	3 med. fat meat
Sandwich Steak	4 oz.	208	2	20	11	*	62	850	3 med. fat meat
Sirloin, Choice	7 oz.	241	1	35	11	*	63	570	5 lean meat
Sirloin Tips, Choice	5 oz.	197	1	29	8	*	71	280	4 lean meat
Steak Kabobs (meat only)	3 oz.	153	2	26	5	*	67	280	3 lean meat
Teriyaki Steak	5 oz.	174	5	32	3	*	64	1420	4 lean meat
T-Bone, Choice	10 oz.	444	2	44	18	*	80	850	6 med. fat meat
T-Bone, Non-graded	8 oz.	277	1	35	9	*	71	850	5 lean meat
Chicken Wings	2 pieces	213	11	11	9	*	75	610	1 starch, 1 med. fat meat, 1 fat
Meatballs	2 pieces	115	2	5	4	*	21	16	1 med. fat meat
Mini Shrimp	6 pieces	47	6	5	1	*	22	125	1 lean meat
Sweet/Sour Sauce	1 oz.	37	8	tr	tr	*	0	80	½ fruit
Breaded Cauliflower	4 oz.	115	23	4	1	*	1	446	1½ starch

🗄 = More than 2 fat exchanges per serving   🏭 = More than 800 milligrams sodium   🛒 = High amounts of sugar

Products	SERVING SIZE	CALORIES	CARBO-HYDRATE (gm)	PROTEIN (gm)	FAT (gm)	SAT. FAT (gm)	CHOLES-TEROL (mg)	SODIUM (mg)	Exchanges
Breaded Okra	4 oz.	124	23	3	1	*	1	483	1½ starch
Breaded Onion Rings	4 oz.	213	30	3	9	*	2	620	2 starch, 2 fat
Breaded Zucchini	4 oz.	102	18	3	1	*	1	584	1 starch
Cheese, Herb, Garlic	1 tbsp.	100	0	0	10	*	0	120	2 fat
Italian Breadsticks	1 each	100	19	4	1	*	0	200	1 starch
Potato Wedges	3.5 oz.	130	16	3	6	*	*	170	1 starch, 1 fat
Rice Pilaf	4 oz.	160	26	4	4	*	22	450	1½ starch, 1 fat
Rolls, Dinner	1 each	184	33	5	3	*	0	311	2 starch, ½ fat
Rolls, Sourdough	1 each	110	22	4	1	*	0	230	1½ starch
Stuffing	4 oz.	230	27	6	11	*	22	800	2 starch, 2 fat
Tortilla Chips	1 oz.	150	16	3	8	*	0	80	1 starch, 2 fat
Spaghetti and Sauce	6 oz.	188	33	5	5	*	0	520	2 starch, 1 med. fat meat
Beans, Baked	4 oz.	170	21	6	6	*	0	330	1½ starch, 1 fat
Beans, Green	3.5 oz.	20	3	1	0	*	0	391	1 vegetable
Carrots	3.5 oz.	31	7	1	0	*	0	33	1 vegetable
Corn	3.5 oz.	90	21	3	0	*	0	5	1½ starch
Peas	3.5 oz.	67	12	5	0	*	0	120	1 starch
Potatoes, Baked	7.2 oz.	145	33	4	0	*	0	6	2 starch
Potatoes, French fried	3 oz.	120	17	2	4	*	3	39	1 starch, 1 fat
Potatoes, Mashed	4 oz.	62	13	2	0	*	20	191	1 starch
Salad Dressings:									
Blue Cheese Dressing	1 oz.	130	1	1	14	*	27	266	3 fat
Cole Slaw Dressing	1 oz.	150	6	tr	14	*	31	284	3 fat
Creamy Italian Dressing	1 oz.	103	3	0	10	*	0	373	2 fat
Parmesan Pepper Dressing	1 oz.	150	2	1	15	*	9	281	3 fat
Ranch Dressing	1 oz.	147	1	tr	15	*	3	297	3 fat
Reduced Calorie Cucumber	1 oz.	69	3	tr	6	*	0	315	1½ fat
Reduced Calorie Italian	1 oz.	31	1	0	3	*	0	371	1 fat
Sweet-n-Tangy Dressing	1 oz.	122	8	tr	10	*	1	347	2 fat
Thousand Island Dressing	1 oz.	113	8	tr	10	*	9	405	2 fat

Products	SERVING SIZE	CALORIES	CARBO-HYDRATE (gm)	PROTEIN (gm)	FAT (gm)	SAT. FAT (gm)	CHOLES-TEROL (mg)	SODIUM (mg)	Exchanges
Salad Bar:									
Lettuce	1 oz.	5	2	0	0	*	0	5	Free
Raw vegetables	1 oz.	9	2	1	0	*	0	3	Free
Cheese, Shredded Imitation	1 oz.	90	1	6	7	*	5	420	1 high fat meat
Chicken Salad	3.5 oz.	212	8	11	15	*	42	334	½ starch, 2 med. fat meat
Croutons	1 oz.	115	18	4	4	*	0	351	1 starch, 1 fat
Eggs, Diced	2 oz.	93	1	7	7	*	260	74	1 med. fat meat
Garbanzo Beans	1 oz.	102	17	6	0	*	0	7	1 starch
Ham, Diced	2 oz.	120	1	9	10	*	76	780	1 med. fat meat, 1 fat
Julienne Turkey	1 oz.	29	1	5	1	*	15	192	1 lean meat
Macaroni Salad	3.5 oz.	335	49	8	12	*	9	431	3 starch, 2 fat
Pasta Salad, pre-made	3.5 oz.	268	34	6	12	*	0	441	2 starch, 2 fat
Potato Salad	3.5 oz.	126	16	2	6	*	7	300	1 starch, 1 fat
Turkey Ham Salad	3.5 oz.	186	10	8	13	*	12	654	1 starch, 1 med. fat meat, 1 fat
Cheese Spread	1 oz.	98	4	4	7	*	26	188	1 high fat meat
Cottage Cheese	4 oz.	120	5	15	5	*	17	330	2 lean meat
Cracker Assortment									
Meal Mate Sesame	2 pieces	45	6	1	2	*	0	95	½ starch
Melba Snacks	4 pieces	36	8	2	0	*	0	60	½ starch
Ritz	2 pieces	40	4	0	2	*	0	50	½ starch
Sesame Breadsticks	2 pieces	35	6	1	0	*	0	60	½ starch

OCCASIONAL USE

Products	SERVING SIZE	CALORIES	CARBO-HYDRATE (gm)	PROTEIN (gm)	FAT (gm)	SAT. FAT (gm)	CHOLES-TEROL (mg)	SODIUM (mg)	Exchanges
Gelatin, Plain	4 oz.	71	17	1	0	*	0	73	1 starch
Mousse, Chocolate	4 oz.	312	28	0	18	*	0	72	2 starch, 3 fat
Mousse, Strawberry	4 oz.	297	25	0	18	*	0	68	2 starch, 3 fat
Wafer, Vanilla	2 cookies	35	6	0	1	*	5	25	½ starch
Yogurt, Fruit	4 oz.	115	23	5	1	*	5	70	1½ starch
Yogurt, Vanilla	4 oz.	110	18	5	2	*	6	75	1½ starch
Banana Pudding	4 oz.	207	27	1	10	*	0	114	2 starch, 2 fat
Ice Milk, Chocolate	3.5 oz.	152	30	4	3	*	22	70	2 starch
Ice Milk, Vanilla	3.5 oz.	150	30	4	3	*	20	58	2 starch
Topping, Caramel	1 oz.	100	26	tr	1	*	2	72	1½ fruit

B = More than 2 fat exchanges per serving   ⊤ = More than 800 milligrams sodium   🛒 = High amounts of sugar

Products	SERVING SIZE	CALORIES	CARBO-HYDRATE (gm)	PROTEIN (gm)	FAT (gm)	SAT. FAT (gm)	CHOLES-TEROL (mg)	SODIUM (mg)	Exchanges
Topping, Chocolate	1 oz.	90	24	tr	tr	*	0	37	1½ fruit
Topping, Strawberry	1 oz.	71	24	tr	tr	*	0	29	1½ fruit
Topping, Whipped	1 oz.	80	5	0	7	*	0	16	2 fat

QUINCY'S FAMILY STEAKHOUSE

Products	SERVING SIZE	CALORIES	CARBO-HYDRATE (gm)	PROTEIN (gm)	FAT (gm)	SAT. FAT (gm)	CHOLES-TEROL (mg)	SODIUM (mg)	Exchanges
Sirloin	Large (218 gm.)	852	0	50	70	*	*	241	7 med. fat meat, 7 fat
Sirloin	Regular (166 gm.)	649	0	38	54	*	*	206	5½ med. fat meat, 5 fat
Sirloin	Petite (114 gm.)	446	0	26	37	*	*	118	4 med. fat meat, 3½ fat
Sirloin Club	1 (137 gm.)	283	0	44	10	*	*	160	6 lean meat
T-Bone, Extra-thick	1 (369 gm.)	1612	0	71	159	*	*	389	10 med. fat meat, 22 fat
Sirloin, Extra-thick	1 (228 gm.)	892	0	52	73	*	*	281	7½ med. fat meat, 8 fat
Ribeye, Extra-thick	1 (270 gm.)	865	0	40	78	*	*	298	6 med. fat meat, 10 fat
Filet, Extra-thick	1 (160 gm.)	331	0	51	12	*	*	159	7 lean meat
Ribeye Steak	1 (208 gm.)	665	0	31	60	*	*	205	4½ med. fat meat, 7½ fat
T-Bone Steak	1 (222 gm.)	1045	0	43	95	*	*	222	6 med. fat meat, 13 fat
Sirloin Tips	1 order (114 gm.)	236	0	37	9	*	*	113	5 lean meat
Chopped Steak	1 (164 gm.)	466	0	40	34	*	*	96	6 med. fat meat, 1 fat
Luncheon Chopped Steak	1 (122 gm.)	350	0	30	25	*	*	72	4 med. fat meat, 1 fat
Country Style Steak w/Mushroom Sauce	1 (171 gm.)	288	17	18	19	*	*	315	1 starch, 2 med. fat meat, 2 fat
Chicken Strips	4 (128 gm.)	318	4	39	15	*	*	*	6 lean meat

Products	SERVING SIZE	CALORIES	CARBO-HYDRATE (gm)	PROTEIN (gm)	FAT (gm)	SAT. FAT (gm)	CHOLES-TEROL (mg)	SODIUM (mg)	Exchanges
Shrimp	7 (110 gm.)	248	11	22	12	*	*	205	1 starch, 3 lean meat
Chili Cheeseburger	1 (381 gm.)	919	46	57	54	*	*	1100	3 starch, 7 med. fat meat, 4 fat
¼ Lb. Hamburger	1 (191 gm.)	403	32	25	19	*	*	284	2 starch, 3 med. fat meat, 1 fat
¼ Lb. Hamburger w/Cheese	1 (204 gm.)	451	32	28	23	*	*	432	2 starch, 3½ med. fat meat, 1 fat
Catfish Filets	2 (198 gm.)	309	19	26	12	*	*	101	1 starch, 3 med. fat meat
Steak Fries	1 order (156 gm.)	426	56	7	21	*	*	90	4 starch, 4 fat
Baked Potato w/out Butter	1 (250 gm.)	181	41	5	tr	*	*	8	2½ starch
Margarine	1 oz. (28 gm.)	204	tr	tr	22	*	*	268	4½ fat
Green Beans	1 (123 gm.)	40	7	2	1	*	*	500	1 vegetable
Cole Slaw	1 order (60 gm.)	60	4	tr	5	*	*	75	1 vegetable, 1 fat
Peppers & Onions	1 order (114 gm.)	80	8	1	5	*	*	11	1 vegetable, 1 fat
Mushroom Sauce	1 order (85 gm.)	27	5	1	tr	*	*	366	1 vegetable
Barbecue Beans	1 order (220 gm.)	296	43	9	13	*	*	1100	3 starch, 2 fat
Texas Toast w/out Butter	1 slice (25 gm.)	73	14	2	tr	*	*	145	1 starch
Country Style Roll	1 (28 gm.)	70	14	2	1	*	*	135	1 starch
Corn Bread	1 piece (55 gm.)	178	28	4	6	*	*	263	2 starch, 1 fat
Chili w/Beans	1 order (260 gm.)	346	32	20	16	*	*	1380	2 starch, 2 med. fat meat, 1 fat
Vegetable Beef Soup	1 order (245 gm.)	78	10	5	2	*	*	1046	1 starch

▉ = More than 2 fat exchanges per serving   ▲ = More than 800 milligrams sodium   🛒 = High amounts of sugar

Products	SERVING SIZE	CALORIES	CARBO-HYDRATE (gm)	PROTEIN (gm)	FAT (gm)	SAT. FAT (gm)	CHOLES-TEROL (mg)	SODIUM (mg)	Exchanges
Clam Chowder	1 order (260 gm.)	198	15	6	14	*	*	1185	1 starch, 3 fat
Cream of Broccoli Soup	1 order (260 gm.)	193	13	3	14	*	*	1045	1 starch, 3 fat

RAX

Products	SERVING SIZE	CALORIES	CARBO-HYDRATE (gm)	PROTEIN (gm)	FAT (gm)	SAT. FAT (gm)	CHOLES-TEROL (mg)	SODIUM (mg)	Exchanges
Roast Beef Sandwich	Large (226 gm.)	570	41	22	35	*	36	1169	3 starch, 2 med. fat meat, 4 fat
Roast Beef Sandwich	Regular (149 gm.)	320	33	20	11	*	36	969	2 starch, 2 med. fat meat
BBC (Beef, Bacon, & Chicken Sandwich)	1 (212 gm.)	720	40	30	49	*	137	1873	3 starch, 3 med. fat meat, 6 fat
Philly Beef & Cheese Sandwich	1 (234 gm.)	470	44	25	22	*	49	1346	3 starch, 2 med. fat meat, 2 fat
Turkey Bacon Club	1 (254 gm.)	670	41	29	43	*	87	1878	3 starch, 3 med. fat meat, 5 fat
Double WB (plain)	1 (160 gm.)	440	33	20	24	*	50	571	2 starch, 2 med. fat meat, 3 fat
BBQ Sandwich	1 (162 gm.)	420	53	21	14	*	24	4664	3½ starch, 2 med. fat meat
Fish Sandwich	1 (198 gm.)	460	58	14	17	*	tr	935	4 starch, 2 med. fat meat, 2 fat
Ham & Swiss Sandwich	1 (224 gm.)	430	42	23	23	*	37	1737	3 starch, 2 med. fat meat, 2 fat
Small Roast Beef Sandwich (Uncle Al)	1 (89 gm.)	260	21	12	14	*	19	562	1½ starch, 1½ med. fat meat, 1 fat
French Fries (Salted)	Regular (3 oz.)	260	33	2	13	*	4	69	2 starch, 2 fat
French Fries (Salted)	Large (4.5 oz.)	390	50	3	20	*	6	104	3 starch, 4 fat
Potatoes: Plain Potato	1 (250 gm.)	270	60	8	tr	*	tr	70	4 starch
Plain Potato w/Margarine	1 (264 gm.)	370	60	8	11	*	tr	170	4 starch, 2 fat

Products	SERVING SIZE	CALORIES	CARBO-HYDRATE (gm)	PROTEIN (gm)	FAT (gm)	SAT. FAT (gm)	CHOLES-TEROL (mg)	SODIUM (mg)	Exchanges
Potato w/ Sour Cream Topping	1 pkg. (350 gm.)	400	65	11	11	*	tr	149	4 starch, 2 fat
Cheese (3 oz.) & Bacon Potato	1 (364 gm.)	780	110	22	28	*	23	910	7 starch, 1 med. fat meat, 4 fat
Cheese (3 oz.) & Broccoli Potato	1 (192 gm.)	760	112	19	26	*	11	489	7 starch, 1 med. fat meat, 4 fat
BBQ Potato (2 oz. Cheese)	1 (406 gm.)	730	104	24	24	*	18	3624	7 starch, 1 med. fat meat, 3 fat
Chili & Cheddar (2 oz.) Potato	1 (406 gm.)	700	101	22	23	*	25	599	7 starch, 1 med. fat meat, 3 fat
Toppings: Liquid Margarine	1 tbsp.	100	tr	tr	11	*	tr	100	2 fat
Sour Topping	3.5 oz.	130	5	3	11	*	tr	79	2 fat
Bacon Bits	.5 oz.	40	tr	5	2	*	12	427	1 fat
Cheese Sauce	3 oz.	370	50	9	15	*	11	313	3 starch, 3 fat
Broccoli	1.5 oz.	16	2	2	tr	*	tr	7	Free
Chili	3 oz.	80	8	8	2	*	18	221	½ starch, 1 lean meat
Diced Onion	.5 oz.	10	1	tr	tr	*	tr	1	Free
BBQ Topping	2.5 oz.	110	10	10	3	*	18	3245	1 starch, 1 lean meat
Drive-Thru Salads: Garden Salad w/out dressing	1 salad	160	4	12	11	*	273	362	1 vegetable, 1 med. fat meat, 1 fat
Chef Salad w/out dressing	1 salad	230	4	22	14	*	322	1048	1 vegetable, 3 med. fat meat
Salad Bar: Alfalfa Sprouts	1 oz.	8	2	tr	tr	*	tr	tr	Free
Applesauce	1 cup	100	26	tr	tr	*	tr	5	1½ fruit
Bacon Bits	.5 oz.	40	tr	5	2	*	12	427	1 fat
Banana Chips	1 oz.	28	25	1	tr	*	tr	1	½ fruit
Beets	1 cup	60	12	2	tr	*	tr	73	1 starch
Broccoli	½ cup	16	2	2	tr	*	tr	7	Free
Cabbage	1 cup	16	4	tr	tr	*	tr	18	Free

⬛ = More than 2 fat exchanges per serving   ⫟ = More than 800 milligrams sodium   🛒 = High amounts of sugar

Products	SERVING SIZE	CALORIES	CARBO-HYDRATE (gm)	PROTEIN (gm)	FAT (gm)	SAT. FAT (gm)	CHOLES-TEROL (mg)	SODIUM (mg)	Exchanges
Carrots	¼ cup	8	2	tr	tr	*	tr	tr	Free
Cauliflower	½ cup	16	2	2	tr	*	tr	6	Free
Celery	1 tbsp.	tr	tr	tr	tr	*	tr	10	Free
Cheddar Cheese Tidbits	1 oz.	160	12	3	11	*	tr	445	1 starch, 2 fat
Shredded Imitation Cheddar Cheese	1 oz.	90	2	6	6	*	6	310	1 high fat meat
Cherry Peppers	1 tbsp.	6	tr	tr	tr	*	tr	180	Free
Chow Mein Noodles	1 oz	140	17	4	6	*	tr	242	1 starch, 1 fat
Coconut	1 oz.	160	15	tr	11	*	tr	tr	1 starch, 2 fat
Cole Slaw	3.5 oz	70	8	1	4	*	tr	187	1 vegetable, 1 fat
Cottage Cheese	1 cup	250	7	33	10	*	47	561	5 lean meat
Crackers (Saltines)	2	16	4	tr	tr	*	tr	70	1/3 starch
Croutons	.5 oz.	40	8	2	tr	*	tr	155	½ starch
Cucumbers	4 slices	2	tr	tr	tr	*	tr	tr	Free
Eggs	1.5 oz.	70	tr	6	5	*	32	267	1 med. fat meat
Garbanzo Beans	½ cup	360	60	20	5	*	26	tr	4 starch, 1 med. fat meat
Gelatin — Strawberry or Lime	½ cup	90	20	2	tr	*	tr	90	1 starch
Grapefruit Sections	1 cup	80	18	2	tr	*	tr	10	1 fruit
Grapes	1 cup	100	25	tr	tr	*	tr	5	1½ fruit
Green Peppers	¼ cup	8	1	tr	tr	*	tr	5	Free
Honeydew Melon	2 pcs.	25	6	tr	tr	*	tr	5	½ fruit
Kidney Beans	1 cup	220	40	14	1	*	tr	8	2½ starch, 1 lean meat
Macaroni Salad	3.5 oz.	160	21	2	7	*	tr	216	1½ starch, 1 fat
Mushrooms	¼ cup	4	tr	tr	tr	*	tr	tr	Free
Onions	¼ cup	12	3	tr	tr	*	tr	3	Free
Pasta Salad	3.5 oz.	80	16	2	1	*	tr	322	1 starch

Products	SERVING SIZE	CALORIES	CARBO-HYDRATE (gm)	PROTEIN (gm)	FAT (gm)	SAT. FAT (gm)	CHOLES-TEROL (mg)	SODIUM (mg)	Exchanges
Peaches	2 slices	16	4	tr	tr	*	tr	tr	Free
Peas	1 oz.	25	4	2	tr	*	tr	35	1 vegetable
Pineapple (Fresh)	1 slice	45	12	tr	tr	*	tr	1	1 fruit
Pineapple (Canned)	3.5 oz.	100	25	tr	tr	*	tr	10	1½ fruit
Potato Salad	1 cup	260	41	7	7	*	7	tr	3 starch, 1 fat
Pudding — Chocolate, Vanilla, or Butterscotch	3.5 oz.	140	20	2	6	*	2	120	1 starch, 1 fat
Sesame Sticks	1 oz.	150	13	3	10	*	tr	405	1 starch, 2 fat
Soynuts	1 oz.	120	5	10	7	*	tr	151	1 high fat meat
Strawberries	2 oz.	18	4	tr	tr	*	tr	tr	Free
Sunflower Seeds w/Raisins	1 oz.	130	6	5	10	*	tr	5	½ fruit, 1 high fat meat
Three Bean Salad	½ cup	100	23	3	tr	*	tr	450	1½ starch
Turkey Bits	2 oz.	70	tr	10	3	*	49	686	1 lean meat
Watermelon	2 pcs.	18	4	tr	tr	*	tr	tr	Free
Dressings: Blue Cheese	1 tbsp.	50	1	tr	5	*	8	110	1 fat
Lite Blue Cheese	1 tbsp.	35	2	tr	3	*	3	240	½ fat
French	1 tbsp.	60	6	tr	4	*	tr	140	1 fat
Lite French	1 tbsp.	40	5	tr	2	*	tr	122	½ fat
Ranch	1 tbsp.	45	tr	tr	5	*	5	103	1 fat
Italian	1 tbsp.	50	3	tr	4	*	tr	159	1 fat
Lite Italian	1 tbsp.	30	1	tr	3	*	5	152	½ fat
Thousand Island	1 tbsp.	70	3	tr	6	*	8	110	1½ fat
Lite Thousand Island	1 tbsp.	40	3	tr	3	*	5	143	1 fat
Oil	1 tbsp.	130	tr	tr	14	*	tr	tr	3 fat
Vinegar	1 tbsp.	2	tr	tr	tr	*	tr	5	Free
Poppy Seed	1 tbsp.	60	5	tr	4	*	6	107	1 fat

▉ = More than 2 fat exchanges per serving   ▼ = More than 800 milligrams sodium   🛒 = High amounts of sugar

Products	SERVING SIZE	CALORIES	CARBO-HYDRATE (gm)	PROTEIN (gm)	FAT (gm)	SAT. FAT (gm)	CHOLES-TEROL (mg)	SODIUM (mg)	Exchanges
Mexican Bar: Banana Pepper Rings	1 tbsp.	2	tr	tr	tr	*	tr	20	Free
Cheese Sauce (Regular)	3.5 oz.	420	58	10	17	*	11	365	4 starch, 3 fat
Cheese Sauce (Nacho)	3.5 oz.	470	57	10	22	*	11	190	4 starch, 4 fat
Olives	3.5 oz.	110	6	tr	10	*	tr	880	2 fat
Refried Beans	3 oz.	120	16	6	4	*	2	375	1 starch, 1 fat
Sour Topping	3.5 oz.	130	5	3	11	*	tr	79	2 fat
Spanish Rice	3.5 oz.	90	20	3	tr	*	tr	442	1 starch
Spicy Meat Sauce	3.5 oz.	80	6	5	4	*	12	751	1 vegetable, 1 fat
Taco Sauce	3.5 oz.	30	6	1	tr	*	tr	806	1 vegetable
Taco Shells	1 shell	40	6	tr	2	*	tr	53	½ starch
Tortillas	1 tort.	110	19	3	2	*	tr	284	1 starch
Tortilla Chips	1 oz.	140	17	2	7	*	tr	100	1 starch, 1½ fat
Pasta Bar: Alfredo Sauce	3.5 oz.	80	12	2	3	*	10	70	1 starch
Chicken Noodle Soup	3.5 oz.	40	8	2	tr	*	10	40	½ starch
Cream of Broccoli Soup	3.5 oz.	50	6	1	2	*	tr	219	½ starch
Parmesan Cheese Substitute	1 oz..	80	2	8	4	*	tr	1000	1 med. fat meat
Pasta Shells	3.5 oz.	170	27	7	4	*	tr	2	2 starch, 1 fat
Pasta/Vegetable Blend	3.5 oz.	100	12	4	4	*	tr	11	1 starch, 1 fat
Rainbow Rotini	3.5 oz.	180	30	6	4	*	2	9	2 starch, 1 fat
Spaghetti	3.5 oz.	140	23	3	4	*	tr	1	1½ starch, 1 fat
Spaghetti Sauce	3.5 oz.	80	19	1	tr	*	tr	635	1 starch
Spaghetti Sauce w/Meat	3.5 oz.	150	12	7	8	*	tr	419	1 starch, 1 high fat meat

OCCASIONAL USE

Chocolate Chip Cookies	1 cookie	130	17	1	6	*	tr	65	1 starch, 1 fat

Products	SERVING SIZE	CALORIES	CARBO-HYDRATE (gm)	PROTEIN (gm)	FAT (gm)	SAT. FAT (gm)	CHOLES-TEROL (mg)	SODIUM (mg)	Exchanges
NOT RECOMMENDED FOR USE									
Chocolate Milkshake	1	560	97	13	13	*	63	239	
Strawberry Milkshake	1	560	97	13	13	*	62	226	
Vanilla Milkshake	1	500	81	13	14	*	58	286	

RED LOBSTER

Note: All 5 oz. serving size are lunch portions, raw weight. Dinner portion is twice as large.

Products	SERVING SIZE	CALORIES	CARBO-HYDRATE (gm)	PROTEIN (gm)	FAT (gm)	SAT. FAT (gm)	CHOLES-TEROL (mg)	SODIUM (mg)	Exchanges
Catfish	5 oz.	170	0	20	10	3	85	50	3 lean meat
Atlantic Cod	5 oz.	100	0	23	1	tr	70	200	3 lean meat
Flounder	5 oz.	100	1	21	1	tr	70	95	3 lean meat
Grouper	5 oz.	110	0	26	1	tr	65	70	3 lean meat
Haddock	5 oz.	110	2	24	1	tr	85	180	3 lean meat
Halibut	5 oz.	110	1	25	1	tr	60	105	3 lean meat
Mackerel	5 oz.	190	1	20	12	4	100	250	3 med. fat meat
Monkfish	5 oz.	110	0	24	1	tr	80	95	3 lean meat
Atlantic Ocean Perch	5 oz.	130	1	24	4	1	75	190	3 lean meat
Pollock	5 oz.	120	1	28	1	tr	90	90	3 lean meat
Red Rockfish	5 oz.	90	0	21	1	tr	85	95	3 lean meat
Red Snapper	5 oz.	110	0	25	1	tr	70	140	3 lean meat
Norwegian Salmon	5 oz.	230	3	27	12	3	80	60	3 med. fat meat
Sockeye Salmon	5 oz.	160	3	28	4	1	50	60	3 lean meat
Blacktip Shark	5 oz.	150	0	35	1	tr	60	90	4 lean meat
Mako Shark	5 oz.	140	0	34	1	tr	100	60	4 lean meat
Lemon Sole	5 oz.	120	1	27	1	tr	65	90	3 lean meat
Swordfish	5 oz.	100	0	17	4	1	100	140	2 lean meat
Tilefish	5 oz.	100	0	20	2	1	80	60	3 lean meat
Rainbow Trout	5 oz.	170	0	23	9	3	90	90	3 lean meat
Yellowfin Tuna	5 oz.	180	0	32	6	2	70	70	4 lean meat

目 = More than 2 fat exchanges per serving   🍸 = More than 800 milligrams sodium   🛒 = High amounts of sugar

Products	SERVING SIZE	CALORIES	CARBO-HYDRATE (gm)	PROTEIN (gm)	FAT (gm)	SAT. FAT (gm)	CHOLES-TEROL (mg)	SODIUM (mg)	Exchanges
Cherrystone Clams	5 oz.	130	11	18	2	tr	80	540	1 starch, 2 lean meat
King Crab Legs	1 lb.	170	6	32	2	tr	100	900	½ starch, 4 lean meat
Snow Crab Legs	1 lb.	150	1	33	2	1	130	1630	4 lean meat
Calamari, Breaded & Fried	5 oz.	360	30	13	21	6	140	1150	2 starch, 1 med. fat meat, 3 fat
Mussels	3 oz.	70	3	9	2	tr	50	150	1 med. fat meat
Oysters	6 raw on half shell	110	11	8	4	2	60	90	1 starch, 1 med. fat meat
Langostino	5 oz.	120	2	26	1	tr	210	410	3 lean meat
Maine Lobster	1¼ lb.	240	5	36	8	2	310	550	5 lean meat
Rock Lobster	1 tail	230	2	49	3	1	200	1090	7 lean meat
Calico Scallops	5 oz.	180	8	32	2	tr	115	260	½ starch, 4 lean meat
Deep Sea Scallops	5 oz.	130	2	26	2	tr	50	260	3 lean meat
Shrimp	8-12 pieces	120	0	25	2	tr	230	110	3 lean meat
Porterhouse Steak	18 oz.	1420	0	61	131	55	290	150	8 high fat meat, 13 fat
Sirloin Steak	7 oz.	570	0	34	48	20	140	85	5 high fat meat, 2 fat
Strip Streak	7 oz.	690	0	29	64	27	140	70	4 high fat meat, 6 fat
Hamburger	1/3 lb.	320	0	27	23	11	105	70	4 med. fat meat
Chicken Breast	4 oz.	120	0	24	3	1	65	60	3 lean meat

ROY ROGERS

Products	SERVING SIZE	CALORIES	CARBO-HYDRATE (gm)	PROTEIN (gm)	FAT (gm)	SAT. FAT (gm)	CHOLES-TEROL (mg)	SODIUM (mg)	Exchanges
Hamburger	1	472	37	26	25	*	64	607	2½ starch, 3 med. fat meat, 2 fat
Small Hamburger	1	222	23	12	9	*	26	336	1½ starch, 1 med. fat meat, 1 fat
Small Cheeseburger	1	275	24	15	13	*	36	558	1½ starch, 1½ med. fat meat, 1 fat
Cheeseburger	1	525	37	29	29	*	76	830	2½ starch, 3 med. fat meat, 3 fat

Products	SERVING SIZE	CALORIES	CARBO-HYDRATE (gm)	PROTEIN (gm)	FAT (gm)	SAT. FAT (gm)	CHOLES-TEROL (mg)	SODIUM (mg)	Exchanges
RR Bar Burger	1	573	38	36	31	*	96	1252	2½ starch, 4 med. fat meat, 2 fat
Bacon Cheeseburger	1	552	31	32	33	*	83	1025	2 starch, 4 med. fat meat, 3 fat
Roast Beef Sandwich	1	350	37	26	11	*	58	732	2½ starch, 3 lean meat
Roast Beef Sandwich w/Cheese	1	403	37	29	15	*	70	954	2½ starch, 3 med. meat
Large Roast Beef Sandwich	1	373	31	35	12	*	82	840	2 starch, 4 lean meat
Large Roast Beef Sandwich w/Cheese	1	427	31	38	17	*	94	1062	2 starch, 5 lean meat
Fish Sandwich	1	514	58	18	24	*	62	857	4 starch, 1 med. fat meat, 3 fat
Express Burger	1	561	42	27	32	*	70	899	3 starch, 3 med. fat meat, 3 fat
Express Cheeseburger	1	613	42	30	37	*	82	1122	3 starch, 3 med. fat meat, 4 fat
Express Bacon Cheeseburger	1	641	36	33	41	*	89	1317	2½ starch, 4 med. fat meat, 4 fat
Chicken Breast	1	412	17	33	24	*	118	609	1 starch, 4 med. fat meat, 1 fat
Chicken Wing	1	192	9	11	13	*	47	285	½ starch, 1½ med. fat meat, 1 fat
Breast & Wing	1	604	25	44	37	*	165	894	2 starch, 5 med. fat meat, 2 fat
Thigh	1	296	12	18	20	*	85	406	1 starch, 2 med. fat meat, 2 fat
Leg	1	140	6	12	8	*	40	190	2 med. fat meat
Thigh & Leg	1	436	17	30	28	*	125	596	1 starch, 4 med. fat meat, 2 fat
Chicken Nuggets	6 pieces	288	21	10	18	*	63	548	1½ starch, 1 med. fat meat, 3 fat
Biscuit	1	231	26	4	12	*	<5	575	2 starch, 2 fat

🯈 = More than 2 fat exchanges per serving   🏮 = More than 800 milligrams sodium   🛒 = High amounts of sugar

Products	SERVING SIZE	CALORIES	CARBO-HYDRATE (gm)	PROTEIN (gm)	FAT (gm)	SAT. FAT (gm)	CHOLES-TEROL (mg)	SODIUM (mg)	Exchanges
Small Fries	3 oz.	238	29	3	12	*	10	122	2 starch, 2 fat
French Fries	4 oz.	320	39	4	16	*	13	165	2½ starch, 3 fat
Large Fries	5.5 oz.	440	54	6	22	*	19	225	3½ starch, 4 fat
Cole Slaw	1	110	11	1	7	*	<5	261	2 vegetable, 1 fat
Crescent Sandwich	1	408	28	13	27	*	207	820	2 starch, 1 med. fat meat, 4 fat
Crescent Sandwich w/Bacon	1	446	28	15	30	*	212	982	2 starch, 1 med. fat meat, 5 fat
Crescent Sandwich w/Sausage	1	564	28	19	42	*	248	1145	2 starch, 2 med. fat meat, 6 fat
Crescent Sandwich w/Ham	1	456	29	20	29	*	227	1243	2 starch, 2 med. fat meat, 4 fat
Crescent Roll	1	287	27	5	18	*	<5	547	2 starch, 3 fat
Egg & Biscuit Platter	1	557	44	18	34	*	417	1020	3 starch, 2 med. fat meat, 4 fat
Egg & Biscuit Platter w/Bacon	1	607	44	21	39	*	424	1236	3 starch, 2 med. fat meat, 5 fat
Egg & Biscuit Platter w/Ham	1	605	44	21	39	*	424	1236	3 starch, 2 med. fat meat, 5 fat
Egg & Biscuit Platter w/Sausage	1	713	44	25	49	*	458	1345	3 starch, 2 med. fat meat, 8 fat
Orange Juice	8 oz.	120	32	2	tr	*	*	*	2 fruit
Lemonade	12 oz.	150	39	tr	tr	*	*	*	2½ fruit
Salad Bar: Bacon Bits	1 Tbsp.	33	2	3	1	*	*	189	½ fat
Sliced Beets	¼ cup	18	4	tr	tr	*	*	162	Free
Broccoli	¼ cup	6	1	1	tr	*	*	6	Free
Shredded Carrots	¼ cup	12	3	tr	tr	*	*	10	Free
Cheddar Cheese	¼ cup	100	tr	7	8	*	15	275	1 high fat meat
Chinese Noodles	¼ cup	55	7	2	3	*	1	113	½ starch, ½ fat
Cucumbers	5-6 slices	4	1	tr	tr	*	*	2	Free
Chopped Eggs	2 Tbsp.	55	1	4	4	*	*	41	1 med. fat meat

Products	SERVING SIZE	CALORIES	CARBO-HYDRATE (gm)	PROTEIN (gm)	FAT (gm)	SAT. FAT (gm)	CHOLES-TEROL (mg)	SODIUM (mg)	Exchanges
Granola	¼ cup	65	9	2	3	*	*	8	½ starch, 1 fat
Green Pepper	2 Tbsp.	3	1	tr	tr	*	*	tr	Free
Lettuce	1 cup	7	1	1	tr	*	*	4	1 vegetable
Macaroni Salad	¼ cup	93	10	2	5	*	*	301	1 starch, 1 fat
Green Peas	¼ cup	28	5	2	tr	*	*	41	1 vegetable
Greek Pasta Salad	¼ cup	159	19	3	9	*	*	328	1 starch, 2 fat
Potato Salad	¼ cup	54	5	1	3	*	*	348	½ starch, 1 fat
Tomatoes	3 slices	20	5	1	tr	*	*	3	1 vegetable
Dressings: Blue Cheese	2 Tbsp.	150	2	2	16	*	*	153	3 fat
Bacon n' Tomato	2 Tbsp.	136	6	tr	12	*	*	150	3 fat
Ranch	2 Tbsp.	155	4	tr	14	*	*	100	3 fat
1,000 Island	2 Tbsp.	160	4	tr	16	*	*	150	3 fat
Lo-Cal Italian	2 Tbsp.	70	2	tr	6	*	*	100	1 fat

OCCASIONAL USE

Products	SERVING SIZE	CALORIES	CARBO-HYDRATE (gm)	PROTEIN (gm)	FAT (gm)	SAT. FAT (gm)	CHOLES-TEROL (mg)	SODIUM (mg)	Exchanges
Strawberry Sundae	1	216	33	6	7	*	23	99	2 starch, 1 fat
Vitari	per oz.	30	7	*	*	*	9	*	½ fruit

NOT RECOMMENDED FOR USE

Products	SERVING SIZE	CALORIES	CARBO-HYDRATE (gm)	PROTEIN (gm)	FAT (gm)	SAT. FAT (gm)	CHOLES-TEROL (mg)	SODIUM (mg)	Exchanges
Cinnamon Rod	1	376	55	5	15	*	*	339	
Cheese Swirls	1	383	54	8	15	*	*	369	
Apple Swirls	1	328	62	5	7	*	*	279	
Pancake Platter w/syrup, butter	1	386	63	5	13	*	51	547	
Pancake Platter w/syrup, butter, bacon	1	436	63	8	17	*	58	763	
Pancake Platter w/syrup, butter, ham	1	434	64	11	15	*	71	969	
Pancake Platter w/syrup, butter, sausage	1	542	63	11	28	*	92	872	

🯅 = More than 2 fat exchanges per serving   🯆 = More than 800 milligrams sodium   🛒 = High amounts of sugar

Products	SERVING SIZE	CALORIES	CARBO-HYDRATE (gm)	PROTEIN (gm)	FAT (gm)	SAT. FAT (gm)	CHOLES-TEROL (mg)	SODIUM (mg)	Exchanges
♥ Hot Fudge Sundae	1	337	53	7	13	*	23	186	
♥ Caramel Sundae	1	293	52	7	9	*	23	193	
♥ Vanilla Shake	1	306	45	8	11	*	40	282	
♥ Chocolate Shake	1	358	61	8	10	*	37	290	
♥ Strawberry Shake	1	315	49	8	10	*	37	261	

SHAKEY'S

Products	SERVING SIZE	CALORIES	CARBO-HYDRATE (gm)	PROTEIN (gm)	FAT (gm)	SAT. FAT (gm)	CHOLES-TEROL (mg)	SODIUM (mg)	Exchanges
Thin Crust Cheese	1/10 12" pizza	133	13	8	5	*	13	323	1 starch, 1 med. fat meat
Thin Crust Pepperoni	1/10 12" pizza	148	13	8	7	*	14	403	1 starch, 1 med. fat meat
Thin Crust Sausage, Pepperoni	1/10 12" pizza	166	13	9	8	*	17	397	1 starch, 1 high fat meat
Thin Crust Sausage, Mushroom	1/10 12" pizza	141	13	9	6	*	13	336	1 starch, 1 med. fat meat
Thin Crust Onion, Green Pepper, Olive, Mushroom	1/10 12" pizza	125	14	7	5	*	11	313	1 starch, 1 med. fat meat
Thin Crust Shakey's Special	1/10 12" pizza	171	14	13	9	*	16	475	1 starch, 2 med. fat meat
Thick Crust Cheese	1/10 12" pizza	170	22	9	5	*	13	421	1½ starch, 1 med. fat meat
Thick Crust Pepperoni	1/10 12" pizza	185	22	10	6	*	17	422	1½ starch, 1 med. fat meat
Thick Crust Sausage, Pepperoni	1/10 12" pizza	177	22	11	8	*	19	424	1½ starch, 1 med. fat meat
Thick Crust Sausage, Mushroom	1/10 12" pizza	179	22	10	6	*	15	420	1½ starch, 1 med. fat meat
Thick Crust Onion, Green Pepper, Mushroom, Olive	1/10 12" pizza	162	22	9	4	*	13	418	1 starch, 1 med fat meat, 1 vegetable
Thick Shakey's Special	1/10 12" pizza	208	22	13	8	*	18	423	1½ starch, 2 med. fat meat

Products	SERVING SIZE	CALORIES	CARBO-HYDRATE (gm)	PROTEIN (gm)	FAT (gm)	SAT. FAT (gm)	CHOLES-TEROL (mg)	SODIUM (mg)	Exchanges
Homestyle — Cheese	1/10 12" pizza	303	31	14	14	*	21	591	2 starch, 1½ med. fat meat, 1 fat
Homestyle — Onion, Green Peppers, Olives, Mushrooms	1/10 12" pizza	320	32	15	14	*	21	652	2 starch, 1½ med. fat meat, 1 fat
Homestyle — Sausage, Pepperoni	1/10 12" pizza	374	31	17	20	*	24	676	2 starch, 2 med. fat meat, 2 fat
Homestyle — Sausage, Mushrooms	1/10 12" pizza	343	31	16	17	*	24	677	2 starch, 2 med. fat meat, 1 fat
Homestyle — Pepperoni	1/10 12" pizza	343	31	16	15	*	27	740	2 starch, 2 med. fat meat, 1 fat
Homestyle — Shakey's Special	1/10 12" pizza	384	32	18	21	*	29	878	2 starch, 2 med. fat meat, 2 fat
Shakey's Super Hot Hero	1	810	67	36	44	*	*	2688	4½ starch, 3 med. fat meat, 6 fat
Hot Ham & Cheese	1	550	56	36	21	*	*	2135	4 starch, 3½ med. fat meat, 1 fat
Fried Chicken & Potatoes	3 pieces	947	51	57	56	*	*	2293	3½ starch, 6 med. fat meat, 5 fat
Potatoes	15 pieces	950	120	17	36	*	*	3703	6 starch, 7 fat
Spaghetti w/Meat Sauce & Garlic Bread	1 order	940	134	26	33	*	*	1904	9 starch, 6 fat

STEAK 'N SHAKE

Products	SERVING SIZE	CALORIES	CARBO-HYDRATE (gm)	PROTEIN (gm)	FAT (gm)	SAT. FAT (gm)	CHOLES-TEROL (mg)	SODIUM (mg)	Exchanges
Steakburger	1 (120.4 gm.)	277	33	18	7	*	*	425	2 starch, 2 lean meat
Steakburger w/Cheese	1 (140.9 gm.)	353	33	23	13	*	*	658	2 starch, 3 med. fat meat
Super Steakburger	1 (165.4 gm.)	375	33	30	12	*	*	447	2 starch, 4 lean meat
Super Steakburger w/Cheese	1 (185.9 gm.)	451	33	35	18	*	*	680	2 starch, 4 med. fat meat

🯳 = More than 2 fat exchanges per serving   🯆 = More than 800 milligrams sodium   🛒 = High amounts of sugar

Products	SERVING SIZE	CALORIES	CARBO-HYDRATE (gm)	PROTEIN (gm)	FAT (gm)	SAT. FAT (gm)	CHOLES-TEROL (mg)	SODIUM (mg)	Exchanges
Triple Steakburger	1 (210.4 gm.)	474	33	43	17	*	*	468	2 starch, 6 lean meat
▼ Triple Steakburger w/Cheese	1 (251.4 gm.)	626	34	52	30	*	*	934	2 starch, 7 med. fat meat
Low Calorie Platter	1 (201.3 gm.)	293	3	37	14	*	*	242	5 lean meat
▼ Baked Ham Sandwich	1 (171.9 gm.)	451	37	29	22	*	*	1858	2½ starch, 3 med. fat meat, 1 fat
Toasted Cheese Sandwich	1 (78.2 gm.)	250	24	9	13	*	*	606	2 starch, 1 med. fat meat, 1 fat
▼ Ham & Egg Sandwich	1 (194.1 gm.)	434	33	36	17	*	*	1850	2 starch, 4 med. fat meat
Egg Sandwich	1 (123.2 gm.)	275	33	12	10	*	*	490	2 starch, 1 med. fat meat, 1 fat
French Fries	1 order (77 gm.)	211	28	3	10	*	*	297	2 starch, 2 fat
▼ Chili & Oyster Crackers	1 order (207.8 gm.)	337	37	16	14	*	*	1157	2½ starch, 2 med. fat meat, 2 fat
▼ Chili Mac & 4 Saltines	1 order (246.8 gm.)	310	34	15	12	*	*	1301	2 starch, 1 med. fat meat, 1 fat
▼ Chili 3 Ways & 4 Saltines	1 order (335.4 gm.)	411	45	19	16	*	*	1734	3 starch, 2 med. fat meat, 1 fat
Baked Beans	1 order (141.6 gm.)	173	27	9	4	*	*	656	2 starch, 1 fat
▌ Lettuce & Tomato Salad w/1 oz. 1000 Island Dressing	1 (96.9 gm.)	168	7	1	15	*	*	223	1 vegetable, 3 fat
▼ Chef Salad	1 (272 gm.)	313	6	41	18	*	*	1582	1 vegetable, 5 lean meat
Cottage Cheese	½ cup (101 gm.)	93	3	12	4	*	*	198	2 lean meat

OCCASIONAL USE

Products	SERVING SIZE	CALORIES	CARBO-HYDRATE (gm)	PROTEIN (gm)	FAT (gm)	SAT. FAT (gm)	CHOLES-TEROL (mg)	SODIUM (mg)	Exchanges
♛ Brownie	1 (70 gm.)	258	39	3	12	*	*	165	2½ starch, 2 fat
Vanilla Ice Cream	1 order (110.4 gm.)	213	23	1	12	*	*	70	1½ starch, 2 fat

Products	SERVING SIZE	CALORIES	CARBO-HYDRATE (gm)	PROTEIN (gm)	FAT (gm)	SAT. FAT (gm)	CHOLES-TEROL (mg)	SODIUM (mg)	Exchanges
NOT RECOMMENDED FOR USE									
Apple Danish	1 (84.7 gm.)	391	35	6	24	*	*	352	
Vanilla Shake	1 (304.9 gm.)	619	58	13	38	*	*	181	
Strawberry Shake	1 (314.9 gm.)	648	62	16	40	*	*	191	
Chocolate Shake	1 (298 gm.)	608	57	13	38	*	*	178	
Orange Freeze	1 (309.9 gm.)	516	63	14	24	*	*	198	
Lemon Freeze	1 (330.9 gm.)	548	69	15	25	*	*	213	
Coca-Cola Float	1 (338 gm.)	514	76	16	17	*	*	230	
Orange Float	1 (330 gm.)	502	74	16	17	*	*	224	
Lemon Float	1 (365 gm.)	555	82	18	19	*	*	248	
Root Beer Float	1 (348 gm.)	529	78	17	17	*	*	237	
Hot Chocolate	1 (175 gm.)	686	129	17	19	*	*	669	
Strawberry Sundae	1 (194.3 gm.)	330	29	2	22	*	*	81	
Hot Fudge Nut Sundae	1 (201.3 gm.)	530	51	5	34	*	*	121	
Brownie Fudge Sundae	1 (224.5 gm.)	645	81	7	35	*	*	262	
Apple Pie	1 (159 gm.)	407	61	4	18	*	*	479	
Cherry Pie	1 (125 gm.)	334	48	6	14	*	*	268	
Apple Pie A La Mode	1 (232.6 gm.)	549	76	4	25	*	*	525	
Cherry Pie A La Mode	1 (198.6 gm.)	476	63	6	22	*	*	314	

▐ = More than 2 fat exchanges per serving   ⊤ = More than 800 milligrams sodium   🛒 = High amounts of sugar

Products	SERVING SIZE	CALORIES	CARBO-HYDRATE (gm)	PROTEIN (gm)	FAT (gm)	SAT. FAT (gm)	CHOLES-TEROL (mg)	SODIUM (mg)	Exchanges
Cheesecake	1 (126 gm.)	368	61	7	11	*	*	294	
Cheesecake w/Strawberries	1 (176 gm.)	386	65	7	11	*	*	294	

TACO BELL

Products	SERVING SIZE	CALORIES	CARBO-HYDRATE (gm)	PROTEIN (gm)	FAT (gm)	SAT. FAT (gm)	CHOLES-TEROL (mg)	SODIUM (mg)	Exchanges
Bean Burrito	1 (191 gm.)	359	54	13	11	5	13	922	3½ starch, 1 med. fat meat, 1 fat
Beef Burrito	1 (191 gm.)	402	38	22	17	8	59	993	2½ starch, 2 med. fat meat, 1 fat
Double Beef Burrito Supreme	1 (255 gm.)	451	40	23	22	10	59	928	3 starch, 2 med. fat meat, 2 fat
Tostada	1 (156 gm.)	243	28	10	11	5	18	670	2 starch, 1 med. fat meat, 1 fat
Beefy Tostada	1 (196 gm.)	322	22	15	20	10	40	764	1½ starch, 1½ med. fat meat, 2 fat
Bellbeefer	1 (177 gm.)	312	32	16	13	6	39	855	2 starch, 1½ med. fat meat, 1 fat
Burrito Supreme	1 (248 gm.)	422	46	17	19	9	35	952	3 starch, 1½ med. fat meat, 2 fat
Combination Burrito	1 (191 gm.)	380	46	17	14	6	36	957	3 starch, 1½ med. fat meat, 1 fat
Enchirito	1 (213 gm.)	382	30	21	20	10	56	1260	2 starch, 2 med. fat meat, 2 fat
Taco	1 (78 gm.)	184	11	10	11	4	32	274	1 starch, 2 lean meat
Taco Light Platter	1 (488 gm.)	1062	97	38	58	34	82	2068	6 starch, 3 med. fat meat, 8 fat
Burrito Supreme Platter	1 (452 gm.)	774	76	35	37	19	79	1920	5 starch, 3 med. meat, 4 fat
Cinnamon Crisps	1 order (47 gm.)	266	20	3	16	13	2	122	2 starch, 3 fat
Taco Sauce	1 packet	2	tr	tr	tr	0	0	126	Free
Salsa	1 packet (10 gm.)	18	4	1	tr	0	0	376	Free
Ranch Dressing	1 packet (74 gm.)	236	1	2	25	5	35	571	5 fat

Products	SERVING SIZE	CALORIES	CARBO-HYDRATE (gm)	PROTEIN (gm)	FAT (gm)	SAT. FAT (gm)	CHOLES-TEROL (mg)	SODIUM (mg)	Exchanges
Guacamole	1 serving (21 gm.)	34	3	tr	2	tr	0	113	½ fat
Taco Salad w/out Beans	1 (516 gm.)	822	47	31	57	38	81	1368	3 starch, 3 med. fat meat, 8 fat
Taco Salad w/out Salsa	1 (510 gm.)	931	60	35	62	40	85	1387	4 starch, 3½ med. fat meat, 8 fat
Taco Salad with Ranch Dressing	1 (584 gm.)	1167	61	37	87	45	121	1959	4 starch, 3½ med. fat meat, 13 fat
Seafood Salad w/Ranch Dressing	1 (435 gm.)	884	49	25	66	34	117	1489	3 starch, 3 med. fat meat, 10 fat
Seafood Salad w/out Dressing/ Shell	1 (291 gm.)	217	12	18	11	6	81	693	1 starch, 2 med. fat meat
Seafood Salad w/out Dressing	1 (362 gm.)	648	47	24	42	30	82	917	3 starch, 2 med. fat meat, 6 fat
Cheesarito	1 (115 gm.)	312	37	12	13	7	29	451	2 starch, 1 med. meat, 2 fat
Mexican Pizza	1 (269 gm.)	714	43	28	48	31	81	1364	3 starch, 3 med. fat meat, 6 fat
Taco Bellgrande Platter	1 (488 gm.)	1002	99	37	51	29	80	1962	6½ starch, 3 med. fat meat, 6 fat
Pintos & Cheese	1 order (127 gm.)	194	19	9	10	5	19	733	1 starch, 1 med. fat meat, 1 fat
Nachos	1 order (106 gm.)	346	37	7	18	6	9	399	2½ starch, 4 fat
Nachos Bellgrande	1 order (287 gm.)	649	61	22	35	12	36	997	4 starch, 2 med. fat meat, 6 fat
Taco Bellgrande	1 (170 gm.)	351	20	18	22	13	55	470	1 starch, 2 med. fat meat, 3 fat
Taco Light	1 (170 gm.)	411	18	19	29	18	57	575	1 starch, 2 med. fat meat, 4 fat
Soft Taco	1 (92 gm.)	228	18	12	12	5	32	516	1 starch, 1½ med. fat meat, 1 fat
Taco Salad w/Salsa	1 (601 gm.)	949	63	36	62	40	86	1763	4 starch, 4 med. fat meat, 8 fat

▤ = More than 2 fat exchanges per serving   ⚓ = More than 800 milligrams sodium   🛒 = High amounts of sugar

Products	SERVING SIZE	CALORIES	CARBO-HYDRATE (gm)	PROTEIN (gm)	FAT (gm)	SAT. FAT (gm)	CHOLES-TEROL (mg)	SODIUM (mg)	Exchanges
Taco Salad w/out Shell	1 (530 gm.)	502	26	29	31	14	80	1056	2 starch, 3 med. fat meat, 3 fat
Taco Salad w/Salsa, w/out Shell	1 (530 gm.)	520	30	31	31	14	80	1431	2 starch, 4 med. fat meat, 2 fat
Fajita Steak Taco	1 (142 gm.)	235	20	15	11	5	14	507	1 starch, 2 med. fat meat
Fajita Steak Taco w/Sour Cream	1 (163 gm.)	281	21	15	15	7	14	507	1 starch, 2 med. fat meat, 1 fat
Fajita Steak Taco w/Guacamole	1 (163 gm.)	269	23	15	13	5	14	620	1 starch, 2 med. fat meat, 1 fat
Chicken Fajita	1 (135 gm.)	226	20	14	10	4	44	619	1 starch, 2 med. fat meat

TCBY (THE COUNTRY'S BEST YOGURT)

Products	SERVING SIZE	CALORIES	CARBO-HYDRATE (gm)	PROTEIN (gm)	FAT (gm)	SAT. FAT (gm)	CHOLES-TEROL (mg)	SODIUM (mg)	Exchanges
TCBY — All flavors	5 oz.	150-169	27-29	4	3-4	*	11-15	65	2 starch

WENDY'S

Products	SERVING SIZE	CALORIES	CARBO-HYDRATE (gm)	PROTEIN (gm)	FAT (gm)	SAT. FAT (gm)	CHOLES-TEROL (mg)	SODIUM (mg)	Exchanges
Single Hamburger Patty on White Bun (¼ lb.)	1 (127 gm.)	350	26	24	16	*	75	360	2 starch, 3 med. fat meat
Double Hamburger Patty on White Bun	1 (203 gm.)	560	26	44	30	*	150	465	2 starch, 6 med. fat meat
Big Classic on Kaiser Bun	1 (241 gm.)	470	36	26	25	*	80	900	2 starch, 3 med. fat meat, 2 fat
Big Classic Double on Kaiser Bun	1 (317 gm.)	680	36	46	39	*	155	1005	2 starch, 6 med. fat meat, 2 fat
Double w/Cheese	1 (221 gm.)	620	26	48	36	*	165	760	2 starch, 6 med. fat meat, 1 fat
Bacon Cheeseburger	1 (151 gm.)	440	26	30	24	*	95	680	2 starch, 3 med. fat meat, 2 fat
Chicken Fried Steak	1 (176 gm.)	580	25	28	41	*	95	1040	2 starch, 3 med. fat meat, 5 fat
Fish Fillet	1 (92 gm.)	210	13	14	11	*	45	475	1 starch, 2 med. fat meat
Multi Grain Bun	1 (48 gm.)	140	25	5	3	*	tr	215	2 starch

Products	SERVING SIZE	CALORIES	CARBO-HYDRATE (gm)	PROTEIN (gm)	FAT (gm)	SAT. FAT (gm)	CHOLES-TEROL (mg)	SODIUM (mg)	Exchanges
Kids' Meal Hamburger	1 (72 gm.)	200	17	13	9	*	35	225	1 starch, 2 med. fat meat
Kaiser Bun	1 (66 gm.)	180	32	7	2	*	5	390	2 starch
White Bun	1 (51 gm.)	140	26	4	2	*	tr	255	2 starch
Chicken Breast on White Bun	1 (138 gm.)	340	30	26	12	*	60	565	2 starch, 3 lean meat
Sandwich Toppings: American Cheese Slice	1 slice	60	tr	4	6	*	15	295	1 med. fat meat
Bacon	1 strip	30	tr	2`	2	*	5	125	1 fat
Ketchup	1 tsp.	6	1	tr	tr	*	0	50	Free
Lettuce	1 leaf	2	tr	tr	tr	*	0	tr	Free
Mayonnaise	1 tbsp.	90	tr	tr	10	*	10	60	2 fats
Mustard	1 tsp.	4	tr	tr	tr	*	0	45	Free
Onion	3 rings	2	tr	tr	tr	*	0	tr	Free
Dill Pickles	4 slices	2	tr	tr	tr	*	0	tr	Free
Tomatoes	1 slice	2	tr	tr	tr	*	0	tr	Free
Plain Baked Potato	1 (250 gm.)	250	52	6	2	*	tr	60	3½ starch
Bacon & Cheese Potato	1 (350 gm.)	570	57	19	30	*	22	1180	3½ starch, 1 med. fat meat, 5 fat
Broccoli & Cheese Potato	1 (365 gm.)	500	54	13	25	*	22	430	3½ starch, 5 fat
Cheese Potato	1 (350 gm.)	590	55	17	34	*	22	450	3½ starch, 1 med. fat meat, 5 fat
Chili & Cheese Potato	1 (400 gm.)	510	63	22	20	*	22	610	4 starch, 1½ med. fat meat, 2 fat
Sour Cream & Chives Potato	1 (310 gm.)	460	53	6	24	*	15	230	3½ starch, 5 fat
Cheese Sauce	2 oz.	140	3	5	12	*	20	415	1 high fat meat, 1 fat
Chives	½ tsp.	8	1	tr	tr	*	0	*	Free
Margarine, Liquid	.5 oz.	100	tr	tr	11	*	0	100	2 fat

▯ = More than 2 fat exchanges per serving   **⊤** = More than 800 milligrams sodium   **🛒** = High amounts of sugar

Products	SERVING SIZE	CALORIES	CARBO-HYDRATE (gm)	PROTEIN (gm)	FAT (gm)	SAT. FAT (gm)	CHOLES-TEROL (mg)	SODIUM (mg)	Exchanges
Margarine, Whipped	1 tbsp.	70	tr	tr	8	*	0	60	2 fat
Sour Cream	2 tsp.	20	tr	tr	2	*	5	5	½ fat
French Fries	Regular	300	35	5	15	*	5	135	2 starch, 3 fat
French Fries	Large	390	46	6	20	*	7	176	3 starch, 4 fat
Cheddar Chips	1 oz. (28 gm.)	160	12	3	11	*	*	445	1 starch, 2 fat
Crispy Chicken Nuggets	6 pieces	310	14	15	21	*	50	660	1 starch, 2 med. fat meat, 2 fat
Chicken Nuggets	9 pieces	465	21	23	32	*	75	990	1½ starch, 3 med. fat meat, 3 fat
Chicken Nuggets	20 pieces	1023	46	50	69	*	160	2178	3 starch, 6 med. fat meat, 8 fat
Barbecue Sauce	1 (28 gm.)	50	11	tr	tr	*	0	100	1 starch or fruit
Sweet & Sour Sauce	1 (28 gm.)	45	11	tr	tr	*	0	55	1 starch or fruit
Sweet Mustard	1 (28 gm.)	50	9	tr	1	*	0	140	1 starch or fruit
Cheese Sauce	2 oz. (963 gm.)	140	3	5	12	*	20	415	3 fat
Tartar Sauce	1 Tbsp. (14 gm.)	80	tr	tr	9	*	*	75	2 fat
Chili	9 oz. (256 gm.)	230	16	21	9	*	50	960	1 starch, 3 lean meat
Taco Salad	1 prepared (791 gm.)	660	46	41	37	*	35	1110	3 starch, 5 med. fat meat, 1 fat
Taco Sauce	1 pkg.	10	tr	tr	tr	*	0	105	Free
Pick-up Window Salad	1 (570 gm.)	110	5	8	6	*	0	540	1 vegetable, 1 fat
Garden Salad (take out)	1 (277 gm.)	102	9	7	5	*	0	110	2 vegetable, 1 fat
Chef Salad (take out)	1 (331 gm.)	180	10	15	9	*	120	140	2 vegetable, 2 med. fat meat
Garden Spot Salad Bar: Lettuce, Iceberg or Romaine	3 cup (165 gm.)	20	3	tr	tr	*	0	20	1 vegetable
	1 cup (55 gm.)	9	1	tr	tr	*	0	5	Free

Products	SERVING SIZE	CALORIES	CARBO-HYDRATE (gm)	PROTEIN (gm)	FAT (gm)	SAT. FAT (gm)	CHOLES-TEROL (mg)	SODIUM (mg)	Exchanges
Cole Slaw	¼ cup (57 gm.)	80	9	tr	5	*	40	165	2 vegetable, 1 fat
Pasta Salad	¼ cup (57 gm.)	130	18	3	6	*	5	190	1 starch, 1 fat
Cottage Cheese	½ cup (105 gm.)	110	3	13	4	*	20	425	2 lean meat
American Cheese	1 oz. (28 gm.)	90	tr	6	7	*	5	365	1 high fat meat
Cheddar Cheese	1 oz. (28 gm.)	90	tr	6	6	*	tr	310	1 high fat meat
Mozzarella Cheese	1 oz. (28 gm.)	90	tr	6	7	*	tr	335	1 high fat meat
Provolone Cheese	1 oz. (28 gm.)	90	tr	6	7	*	tr	335	1 high fat meat
Swiss Cheese	1 oz. (28 gm.)	90	tr	6	7	*	5	365	1 high fat meat
Turkey Ham	¼ cup (36 gm.)	50	tr	6	2	*	*	*	1 lean meat
Bread Sticks	2 (8 gm.)	35	6	1	1	*	0	60	½ starch
Alfalfa Sprouts	1 oz. (28 gm.)	8	tr	1	tr	*	0	tr	Free
Blueberries	1 Tbsp. (9 gm.)	6	1	1	tr	*	0	tr	Free
Broccoli	½ cup (43 gm.)	12	2	2	tr	*	0	5	Free
Red Cabbage	¼ cup (17 gm.)	4	tr	2	tr	*	0	5	Free
Carrots	¼ cup (37 gm.)	tr	2	2	tr	*	0	15	Free
Cauliflower	½ cup (57 gm.)	12	2	1	tr	*	0	10	Free
Celery	1 Tbsp. (7 gm.)	0	tr	1	tr	*	0	5	Free
Cherry Peppers (mild)	1 Tbsp. (14 gm.)	6	tr	1	tr	*	0	180	Free

目 = More than 2 fat exchanges per serving   **⊤** = More than 800 milligrams sodium   **🛒** = High amounts of sugar

Products	SERVING SIZE	CALORIES	CARBO-HYDRATE (gm)	PROTEIN (gm)	FAT (gm)	SAT. FAT (gm)	CHOLES-TEROL (mg)	SODIUM (mg)	Exchanges
Cucumbers	4 slices (14 gm.)	2	tr	1	tr	*	0	tr	Free
Grapefruit	2 oz. (56 gm.)	10	2	0	tr	*	0	0	Free
Green Pepper	¼ cup (37 gm.)	3	1	1	tr	*	0	5	Free
Jalapeno Peppers	1 slice (14 gm.)	9	2	tr	tr	*	0	4	Free
Mushrooms	¼ cup (17 gm.)	4	tr	1	tr	*	0	tr	Free
Pepper Rings	1 Tbsp. (14 gm.)	2	tr	tr	tr	*	0	200	Free
Radishes	.5 oz. (14 gm.)	2	tr	1	tr	*	0	tr	Free
Red Onions	3 Rings (9 gm.)	2	tr	1	tr	*	0	tr	Free
Tomatoes	1 oz. (28 gm.)	6	1	1	tr	*	0	5	Free
Bacon Bits	⅛ oz. (3.5 gm.)	10	tr	1	tr	*	tr	100	Free
Chow Mein Noodles	.5 oz. (14 gm.)	70	8	1	4	*	*	105	½ starch, ½ fat
Croutons	.5 oz. (14 gm.)	70	8	1	4	*	*	105	½ starch, ½ fat
Cantaloupe	2 pieces (57 gm.)	18	4	tr	tr	*	0	5	½ fruit
Grapes	¼ cup (40 gm.)	30	7	tr	tr	*	0	tr	½ fruit
Green Peas	1 oz.	25	4	1	tr	*	0	35	½ starch
Honeydew Melon	2 pieces (57 gm.)	20	5	tr	tr	*	0	5	½ fruit
Oranges	2 oz. (56 gm.)	25	7	tr	tr	*	0	0	½ fruit
Peaches	2 pieces (57 gm.)	17	4	tr	tr	*	0	0	½ fruit
Strawberries	2 oz. (56 gm.)	18	4	tr	tr	*	0	tr	½ fruit

Products	SERVING SIZE	CALORIES	CARBO-HYDRATE (gm)	PROTEIN (gm)	FAT (gm)	SAT. FAT (gm)	CHOLES-TEROL (mg)	SODIUM (mg)	Exchanges
Watermelon	3 pieces (57 gm.)	18	4	tr	tr	*	0	tr	½ fruit
Eggs (hard cooked)	1 Tbsp. (20 gm.)	30	tr	3	2	*	90	25	½ med. fat meat
Parmesan Cheese	1 oz. (30 gm.)	130	1	12	9	*	20	510	1½ med. fat meat
Pineapple Chunks	½ cup (150 gm.)	70	18	tr	tr	*	0	0	1 fruit
Sunflower Seeds & Raisins	1 oz. (28 gm.)	140	6	5	10	*	0	5	½ fruit, 1 high fat meat
Salad Dressings (1 ladle equals 2 tablespoons): Bleu Cheese	1 Tbsp. (15 gm.)	60	1	tr	7	*	10	85	1½ fat
Celery Seed	1 Tbsp. (15 gm.)	70	3	tr	6	*	5	65	1½ fat
French Style	1 Tbsp. (16 gm.)	70	5	tr	5	*	0	130	1½ fat
Golden Italian	1 Tbsp. (16 gm.)	50	3	tr	4	*	0	260	1½ fat
Ranch	1 Tbsp. (15 gm.)	50	2	tr	6	*	5	95	1½ fat
1000 Island	1 Tbsp. (15 gm.)	70	tr	tr	7	*	10	115	1½ fat
Oil	1 Tbsp. (14 gm.)	120	tr	tr	14	*	0	0	3 fat
Wine Vinegar	1 Tbsp. (15 gm.)	2	tr	tr	tr	*	0	5	Free
Reduced Calorie Dressings: Bacon/Tomato	1 Tbsp. (15 gm.)	45	2	tr	4	*	tr	180	1 fat
Creamy Cucumber	1 Tbsp. (15 gm.)	50	2	tr	5	*	tr	140	1 fat
Italian	1 Tbsp. (15 gm.)	25	2	tr	2	*	0	180	1 fat
1000 Island	1 Tbsp. (15 gm.)	45	2	tr	4	*	5	125	1 fat

目 = More than 2 fat exchanges per serving   ⚲ = More than 800 milligrams sodium   🛒 = High amounts of sugar

Products	SERVING SIZE	CALORIES	CARBO-HYDRATE (gm)	PROTEIN (gm)	FAT (gm)	SAT. FAT (gm)	CHOLES-TEROL (mg)	SODIUM (mg)	Exchanges
Old Fashioned Corn Relish	¼ cup (57 gm.)	35	9	tr	tr	*	*	215	1 vegetable
Deluxe Three Bean Salad	¼ cup (57 gm.)	60	13	1	tr	*	*	15	1 starch
Red Bliss Potato Salad	¼ cup (57 gm.)	110	6	tr	9	*	*	265	1 vegetable, 2 fat
Pasta Deli Salad	¼ cup (57 gm.)	35	6	2	tr	*	*	120	1 vegetable
California Coleslaw	2 oz. (57 gm.)	60	9	tr	6	*	10	140	2 vegetable, 1 fat
Omelet, Ham, Cheese and/or Mushroom	1 (114 gm.)	290	7	18	21	*	355	570	1 vegetable, 2½ med fat meat, 2 fat
Omelet, Mushroom, Green Pepper, Onion	1 (114 gm.)	210	7	14	15	*	460	200	1 vegetable, 2 med. fat meat, 1 fat
Omelet, Ham, Cheese, Onion, Green Pepper	1 (128 gm.)	280	7	19	19	*	525	485	1 vegetable, 2½ med. fat meat, 2 fat
Breakfast Sandwich	1 (129 gm.)	370	33	17	19	*	200	770	2 starch, 2 med. fat meat, 2 fat
Breakfast Sandwich w/Sausage	1	570	33	25	37	*	*	1175	2 starch, 2½ med. fat meat, 5 fat
Breakfast Sandwich w/Bacon	1	430	33	21	23	*	*	1020	2 starch, 2 med. fat meat, 3 fat
French Toast	2 slices (135 gm.)	400	45	11	19	*	115	850	3 starch, 4 fat
Apple Topping	1 (70 gm.)	130	32	tr	tr	*	0	120	2 fruit
Blueberry Topping	1 (70 gm.)	60	15	tr	tr	*	0	65	1 fruit
Breakfast Potatoes	1 serving (103 gm.)	360	37	4	22	*	20	745	2½ starch, 4 fat
Buttermilk Biscuit	1 (94 gm.)	320	37	5	17	*	tr	860	2½ starch, 3 fat
Sausage Patty	1 (45 gm.)	200	tr	8	18	*	45	405	1 high fat meat, 2 fat

Products	SERVING SIZE	CALORIES	CARBO-HYDRATE (gm)	PROTEIN (gm)	FAT (gm)	SAT. FAT (gm)	CHOLES-TEROL (mg)	SODIUM (mg)	Exchanges
Sausage Gravy	6 oz. (214 gm.)	440	13	17	36	*	85	1300	1 starch, 2 med. fat meat, 5 fat
Eggs — Scrambled	2 eggs (91 gm.)	190	7	14	12	*	450	160	2 med. fat meat
Bacon	1 strip (6 gm.)	30	tr	2	2	*	5	125	1 fat
Orange Juice	6 oz. (185 gm.)	80	19	1	tr	*	0	tr	1 fruit
White toast	2 slices (69 gm.)	250	35	6	9	*	20	410	2 starch, 2 fat

OCCASIONAL USE

Products	SERVING SIZE	CALORIES	CARBO-HYDRATE (gm)	PROTEIN (gm)	FAT (gm)	SAT. FAT (gm)	CHOLES-TEROL (mg)	SODIUM (mg)	Exchanges
Chocolate Pudding	¼ cup (57 gm.)	90	12	tr	4	*	tr	70	1 starch
Butterscotch Pudding	¼ cup (57 gm.)	90	11	1	4	*	tr	85	1 starch
Syrup	1 Pkg. (425 gm.)	140	37	tr	tr	*	0	5	2 fruit

NOT RECOMMENDED FOR USE

Products	SERVING SIZE	CALORIES	CARBO-HYDRATE (gm)	PROTEIN (gm)	FAT (gm)	SAT. FAT (gm)	CHOLES-TEROL (mg)	SODIUM (mg)	Exchanges
Cheese or Cinnamon Raisin Danish	95 gm.	430	52	8	21	*	*	550	
Apple Danish	95 gm.	360	53	6	14	*	*	380	
Frosty Dairy Dessert	Small (243 gm.)	400	59	8	14	*	50	220	
Frosty Dairy Dessert	Large (413 gm.)	680	100	14	24	*	*	374	
Chocolate Chip Cookie	1 (64 gm.)	320	40	3	17	*	5	325	

WHATABURGER

Products	SERVING SIZE	CALORIES	CARBO-HYDRATE (gm)	PROTEIN (gm)	FAT (gm)	SAT. FAT (gm)	CHOLES-TEROL (mg)	SODIUM (mg)	Exchanges
Whataburger	1 (302 gm.)	580	58	32	24	*	70	1092	4 starch, 3 med. fat meat, 2 fat
Whataburger w/Cheese	1 (326 gm.)	669	58	36	33	*	96	1474	4 starch, 3½ med. fat meat, 3 fat

☷ = More than 2 fat exchanges per serving   ⊤ = More than 800 milligrams sodium   🛒 = High amounts of sugar

Products	SERVING SIZE	CALORIES	CARBO-HYDRATE (gm)	PROTEIN (gm)	FAT (gm)	SAT. FAT (gm)	CHOLES-TEROL (mg)	SODIUM (mg)	Exchanges
Whataburger Jr.	1 (153 gm.)	304	31	15	14	*	30	684	2 starch, 1 med. fat meat, 2 fat
Whataburger Jr. w/Cheese	1 (165 gm.)	351	30	17	18	*	42	921	2 starch, 1 med. fat meat, 3 fat
Justaburger	1 (117 gm.)	265	28	12	12	*	25	547	2 starch, 1 med. fat meat, 1 fat
Justaburger w/Cheese	1 (129 gm.)	312	28	15	16	*	37	784	2 starch, 1 med. fat meat, 2 fat
Whatacatch	1 (177 gm.)	475	43	14	27	*	34	722	3 starch, 1 med. fat meat, 4 fat
Whatacatch w/Cheese	1 (189 gm.)	522	43	16	32	*	45	959	3 starch, 1 med. fat meat, 5 fat
Whataburger Double Meat	1 (385 gm.)	806	59	51	41	*	154	1296	4 starch, 5 med. fat meat, 2 fat
Whataburger Double Meat w/Cheese	1 (409 gm.)	895	59	55	49	*	180	1678	4 starch, 6½ med. fat meat, 3 fat
French Fries	Small	221	25	4	12	*	tr	50	1½ starch, 1 fat
French Fries	Regular	332	37	5	18	*	tr	45	2½ starch, 3 fat
Onions Rings	1 order (72 gm.)	226	22	4	13	*	tr	410	1½ starch, 3 fat
Taquito	1 (125 gm.)	310	17	19	19	*	223	712	1 starch, 2 med. fat meat, 2 fat
Taquito w/Cheese	1 (137 gm.)	357	17	21	23	*	235	949	1 starch, 3 med. fat meat, 1 fat
Taquito Ranchero	1 (153 gm.)	320	19	19	18	*	223	1092	1 starch, 2 med. fat meat, 2 fat
Taquito Ranchero w/Cheese	1 (165 gm.)	367	19	21	23	*	235	1329	1 starch, 2 med. fat meat, 3 fat
Egg Omelette Sandwich	1 (120 gm.)	312	29	14	15	*	191	696	2 starch, 1 med. fat meat, 2 fat
Egg Omelette Sandwich Ranchero	1 (148 gm.)	322	31	15	16	*	191	1067	2 starch, 1 med. fat meat, 2 fat
Pancakes w/out Syrup & Butter	1 order	288	54	9	4	*	49	977	3½ starch, 1 fat
Sausage	1 order	208	1	9	19	*	43	355	1 high fat meat, 2 fat

Products	SERVING SIZE	CALORIES	CARBO-HYDRATE (gm)	PROTEIN (gm)	FAT (gm)	SAT. FAT (gm)	CHOLES-TEROL (mg)	SODIUM (mg)	Exchanges
Breakfast on a Bun	1 (175 gm.)	520	29	23	34	*	234	1051	2 starch, 2 med. fat meat, 5 fat
Breakfast on a Bun Ranchero	1 (203 gm.)	530	32	23	35	*	236	1431	2 starch, 2 med. fat meat, 5 fat
Whatachicken Sandwich	1 (10 oz.)	671	61	35	32	*	71	1460	4 starch, 3 med. fat meat, 3 fat
Ground Beef Patty	¼ lb.	226	1	19	17	*	84	232	3 med. fat meat
Ground Beef Patty	1/10 lb.	90	tr	8	6	*	34	81	1 high fat meat
Bun	5 inch	290	56	10	3	*	tr	532	4 starch
Bun	4 inch	150	29	5	2	*	tr	274	2 starch
Fajita Taco	1 (169 gm.)	301	27	23	11	*	55	1070	2 starch, 2 med. fat meat

OCCASIONAL USE

Products	SERVING SIZE	CALORIES	CARBO-HYDRATE (gm)	PROTEIN (gm)	FAT (gm)	SAT. FAT (gm)	CHOLES-TEROL (mg)	SODIUM (mg)	Exchanges
Apple Pie	1	236	30	3	12	*	tr	265	2 starch, 2 fat
Pecan Danish	1	270	28	5	16	*	12	419	2 starch, 3 fat

NOT RECOMMENDED FOR USE

Products	SERVING SIZE	CALORIES	CARBO-HYDRATE (gm)	PROTEIN (gm)	FAT (gm)	SAT. FAT (gm)	CHOLES-TEROL (mg)	SODIUM (mg)	Exchanges
Vanilla Shake	Small	322	50	9	9	*	37	169	
Vanilla Shake	Medium	439	68	12	13	*	51	230	
Vanilla Shake	Large	657	102	19	19	*	75	874	
Vanilla Shake	Extra Large	877	137	25	26	*	100	1168	

WHITE CASTLE

Products	SERVING SIZE	CALORIES	CARBO-HYDRATE (gm)	PROTEIN (gm)	FAT (gm)	SAT. FAT (gm)	CHOLES-TEROL (mg)	SODIUM (mg)	Exchanges
Hamburger	1 (2 oz.)	161	15	6	8	*	*	266	1 starch, 1 high fat meat
Cheeseburger	1 (2.3 oz.)	200	15	8	11	*	*	361	1 starch, 1 high fat meat, 1 fat
Fish w/out Tartar Sauce	1 (2.1 oz.)	155	21	6	5	*	*	201	1½ starch, ½ high fat meat
Sausage & Egg Sandwich	1 order (3.4 oz.)	322	16	13	22	*	*	698	1 starch, 2 med. fat meat, 2 fat

🯅 = More than 2 fat exchanges per serving   🍼 = More than 800 milligrams sodium   🛒 = High amounts of sugar

Products	SERVING SIZE	CALORIES	CARBO-HYDRATE (gm)	PROTEIN (gm)	FAT (gm)	SAT. FAT (gm)	CHOLES-TEROL (mg)	SODIUM (mg)	Exchanges
Sausage Sandwich	1 (1.7 oz.)	196	13	7	12	*	*	488	1 starch, 1 med. fat meat, 1 fat
Chicken Sandwich	1 (2.3 oz.)	186	21	8	7	*	*	497	1½ starch, 1 med. fat meat
ᗺ French Fries	1 order (3.4 oz.)	301	38	2	15	*	*	193	2½ starch, 3 fat
Onion Rings	1 order (2.1 oz.)	245	27	3	13	*	*	566	2 starch, 2 fat
ᗺ Onion Chips	1 order (3.3 oz.)	329	39	4	17	*	*	832	2½ starch, 3 fat

ZANTIGO

Products	SERVING SIZE	CALORIES	CARBO-HYDRATE (gm)	PROTEIN (gm)	FAT (gm)	SAT. FAT (gm)	CHOLES-TEROL (mg)	SODIUM (mg)	Exchanges
Taco	1 (84.5 gm.)	198	13	10	12	*	*	318	1 starch, 1 med. fat meat, 1 fat
Taco Burrito	1 (198.7 gm.)	415	41	21	19	*	*	815	2½ starch, 2 med. fat meat, 2 fat
Mild Cheese Chilito	1 (115 gm.)	330	36	14	15	*	*	505	2 starch, 1 med. fat meat, 2 fat
Hot Cheese Chilito	1 (115.3 gm.)	329	35	14	15	*	*	466	2 starch, 1 med. fat meat, 2 fat
⊥ Beef Enchilada	1 (184.1 gm.)	315	26	18	15	*	*	904	1½ starch, 2 med. fat meat, 1 fat
ᗺ Cheese Enchilada	1 (179.8 gm.)	390	26	20	23	*	*	759	1½ starch, 2 med. fat meat, 2½ fat

Products	SERVING SIZE	CALORIES	CARBO-HYDRATE (gm)	PROTEIN (gm)	FAT (gm)	SAT. FAT (gm)	CHOLES-TEROL (mg)	SODIUM (mg)	American Exchanges

IN CANADA:

To convert American exchanges to Canadian exchanges, see chart on page 106.

HARVEY'S FOODS

Products	SERVING SIZE	CALORIES	CARBO-HYDRATE (gm)	PROTEIN (gm)	FAT (gm)	SAT. FAT (gm)	CHOLES-TEROL (mg)	SODIUM (mg)	American Exchanges
Hamburger	1	355	40	18	14	*	17	*	3 starch, 2 med. fat meat
Cheeseburger	1	415	41	22	18	*	30	*	3 starch, 2½ med. fat meat
Double Burger	1	530	44	31	26	*	34	*	3 starch, 3 med. fat meat, 2 fat
Super Burger	1	477	38	37	19	*	112	*	2½ starch, 4 med. fat meat
Hot Dog	1	332	32	12	15	*	50	*	2 starch, 1 high fat meat, 2 fat
Chicken Sandwich	1	419	46	19	16	*	110	*	3 starch, 2 med. fat meat, 1 fat
Chicken Fingers	5	240	18	15	12	*	57	*	1 starch, 2 med. fat meat
French Fries	1 order	478	56	10	24	*	5	*	4 starch, 4 fat
Onion Rings	1 order	288	36	4	14	*	5	*	2 starch, 3 fat
Salad	1 serving	33	7	3	tr	*	tr	*	1 vegetable
Dressing	1 order	60	3	tr	5	*	tr	*	1 fat
Western Sandwich	1	347	58	15	10	*	265	*	4 starch, 1 med. fat meat
Egg	1	83	1	5	6	*	246	*	1 med. fat meat
Bacon	3 slices	150	tr	7	14	*	15	*	1 med. fat meat, 2 fat
Breakfast Sausage	1 order	167	3	9	14	*	12	*	1 med. fat meat, 2 fat
Hash Brown	1 order	146	15	2	9	*	2	*	1 starch, 2 fat
Toast Plain	1 order	250	48	8	3	*	tr	*	3 starch
Pancake	1 order	89	17	2	1	*	8	*	1 starch
Muffin Bran	1	301	42	5	13	*	tr	*	3 starch, 2 fat
Muffin Blueberry	1	254	45	4	6	*	tr	*	3 starch, 1 fat

▐ = More than 2 fat exchanges per serving   ⊤ = More than 800 milligrams sodium   🛒 = High amounts of sugar

Products	SERVING SIZE	CALORIES	CARBO-HYDRATE (gm)	PROTEIN (gm)	FAT (gm)	SAT. FAT (gm)	CHOLES-TEROL (mg)	SODIUM (mg)	American Exchanges
Orange Juice	1 order	77	18	1	1	*	tr	*	1 fruit
Apple Juice	1 order	80	20	2	2	*	tr	*	1 fruit
OCCASIONAL USE									
Apple Turnover	1	179	28	1	7	*	7	*	2 starch, 1 fat
NOT RECOMMENDED FOR USE									
Pancake Syrup	1 pkg.	168	43	tr	tr	*	tr	*	
Chocolate Milkshake	1	321	74	12	11	*	36	*	
Vanilla Milkshake	1	305	69	11	10	*	36	*	
Strawberry Milkshake	1	303	69	11	10	*	36	*	
Ice Burger	1	305	43	4	18	*	37	*	

SWISS CHALET

Products	SERVING SIZE	CALORIES	CARBO-HYDRATE (gm)	PROTEIN (gm)	FAT (gm)	SAT. FAT (gm)	CHOLES-TEROL (mg)	SODIUM (mg)	American Exchanges
Chicken White	Quarter chicken	308	tr	35	19	*	*	*	5 lean meat, 1 fat
Chicken Dark	Quarter chicken	326	tr	37	20	*	*	*	5 lean meat, 1 fat
Chicken	Half chicken	634	1	72	38	*	*	*	10 lean meat, 2 fat
Chicken Sandwich	1	360	42	33	5	*	*	*	3 starch, 3 lean meat
Chalet Sauce	1 pkg	20	4	tr	tr	*	*	*	Free
Roll	1	116	24	3	1	*	*	*	1½ starch
Chicken Salad	1	500	23	42	42	*	*	*	1½ starch, 5½ med. fat meat, 2 fat
French Fried Potatoes	1 order	478	57	10	24	*	*	*	4 starch, 4 fat
Baked Potato	1	227	52	8	tr	*	*	*	3½ starch
Chicken Sandwich (Hot)	1	310	30	30	6	*	*	*	2 starch, 3 lean meat
Sandwich Gravy	1 order	35	5	1	1	*	*	*	½ starch

Products	SERVING SIZE	CALORIES	CARBO-HYDRATE (gm)	PROTEIN (gm)	FAT (gm)	SAT. FAT (gm)	CHOLES-TEROL (mg)	SODIUM (mg)	American Exchanges
Peas	1 order	44	7	tr	tr	*	*	*	1 vegetable
Chalet Chicken Soup	1 order	97	11	9	2	*	*	*	1 starch, 1 lean meat
Chalet Salad	1	240	14	tr	20	*	*	*	1 starch, 4 fat
Chalet Cole Slaw	1 order	56	10	2	1	*	*	*	2 vegetable

NOT RECOMMENDED FOR USE

Products	SERVING SIZE	CALORIES	CARBO-HYDRATE (gm)	PROTEIN (gm)	FAT (gm)	SAT. FAT (gm)	CHOLES-TEROL (mg)	SODIUM (mg)	American Exchanges
Apple Pie	1	394	45	3	23	*	*	*	
Fudge Nut Cake	1 piece	346	48	4	16	*	*	*	
Black Forest Cake	1 piece	278	36	3	14	*	*	*	
Coconut Pie	1 piece	292	40	2	14	*	*	*	
Chocolate Eclair	1	205	27	2	10	*	*	*	
Vanilla Ice Cream	1 order	195	16	3	14	*	*	*	
Chocolate Syrup	1 order	104	26	tr	tr	*	*	*	
Butterscotch Syrup	1 order	107	25	tr	tr	*	*	*	

▌ = More than 2 fat exchanges per serving   ⚱ = More than 800 milligrams sodium   🛒 = High amounts of sugar

Comparison of American and Canadian Food Group Systems

American Diabetes Association Exchange System		Canadian Diabetes Association Choice System
1 Starch	=	1 Starchy Foods
1 Lean Meat	=	1 Protein Foods
1 Medium-Fat Meat	=	1 Protein + ½ Fats & Oils
1 High-Fat Meat	=	1 Protein + 1 Fats & Oils
1 Vegetable	=	½ Fruits & Vegetables
(no equivalent)	=	Extra Vegetables
1 Fruit	=	1½ Fruits & Vegetables
1 Milk	=	2 Milk(Skim)
1 Fat	=	1 Fats & Oils

Canadian Diabetes Association.
Comparison of American and Canadian food group systems.
Diabetes Dialogue, 1988; 35 (4): 57.

If you found this book helpful and would like more information on this and other related subjects, you may be interested in one or more of the following titles from our Wellness and Nutrition Library:

BOOKS
Fast Food Facts, 3rd Edition: Nutrition and Exchange Values for Fast Food Restaurants (200 pages)
Fast Food Facts, pocket edition (184 pages)
Making the Most of Medicare: A Personal Guide Through the Medicare Maze (170 pages)
Fight Fat & Win: How to Eat a Low-Fat Diet Without Changing Your Lifestyle (200 pages)
The Guiltless Gourmet Cooks Ethnic: Low-Fat Ethnic Recipes, Menus & Nutrition Facts (250 pages)
When a Family Gets Diabetes: Art Therapy to Help Kids and Families Understand Diabetes (50 pages)
Expresslane Diet: Weight Loss with Convenience and Fast Foods (176 pages)
Retirement: New Beginnings, New Challenges, New Successes (140 pages)
Whole Parent/Whole Child: Raising a Chronically Ill Child (175 pages)
Diabetes: A Guide to Living Well: A Program of Individualized Self-Care (396 pages)
Adult Braces in a Gourmet World: A Consumer's Guide to Straight Teeth (148 pages)
I Can Cope: Staying Healthy with Cancer (202 pages)
Managing the School Age Child with a Chronic Health Condition (350 pages)
Pass the Pepper Please: Healthy Meal Planning with Low Sodium (66 pages)
The Guiltless Gourmet: Recipes, Menus for the Health Conscious Cook (170 pages)
The Joy of Snacks: Good Nutrition for People Who Like to Snack (270 pages)
Convenience Food Facts: Help for the Healthy Meal Planner (188 pages)
Learning to Live Well with Diabetes: Your Complete Guide to Diabetes Management (392 pages)
The Physician Within: Taking Charge of Your Well-Being (170 pages)
Exchanges for All Occasions: Meeting the Challenge of Diabetes and Weight Control (250 pages)
Managing Type II Diabetes: Your Invitation to a Healthier Lifestyle (170 pages)
Diabetes 101: A Pure and Simple Guide for People Who Use Insulin (110 pages)

BOOKLETS & PAMPHLETS
Eating with Food Choices (40 pages)
A Guide to Healthy Eating (60 pages)
Diabetes & Exercise (20 pages)
Emotional Adjustment to Diabetes (16 pages)
A Step in Time: Diabetes Foot Care (18 pages)
Diabetes Record Book (68 pages)
Diabetes & Brief Illness (8 pages)
Adding Fiber to Your Diet (10 pages)
Gestational Diabetes: Guidelines for a Safe Pregnancy (24 pages)
Recognizing and Treating Insulin Reactions (4 pages)

PROFESSIONAL SERIES
Manual of Clinical Nutrition (540 pages)
Simplified Learning Series, 17-booklet preview packet
Diabetes Youth Curriculum: For working with Young Patients, Ages 6 to 16

The Wellness and Nutrition Library is published by Diabetes Center, Inc., in Minneapolis, MN, publishers of quality educational materials dealing with health, wellness, nutrition, diabetes, and other chronic illnesses. All of our books and materials are available nationwide and in Canada through leading bookstores. If you can't find our books at your favorite bookstore, contact us for a free catalog.

DCI Publishing, Inc.
P.O. Box 739
Wayzata, MN 55391